Ancient Society and History

The Origins
in Ancient

The Origins of Rhetoric in Ancient Greece

THOMAS COLE

of Rhetoric Greece

The Johns Hopkins University Press
Baltimore and London

This book has been brought to publication with the generous assistance of the David M. Robinson Fund.

Johns Hopkins Paperbacks edition, 1995
04 03 02 01 00 99 98 97 96 95   5 4 3 2 1

The Johns Hopkins University Press
2715 North Charles Street
Baltimore, Maryland 21218-4319
The Johns Hopkins Press Ltd., London

Library of Congress Cataloging-in-Publication Data
Cole, Thomas, 1933–
    The origins of rhetoric in ancient Greece / Thomas Cole.
        p.   cm. — (Ancient society and history)
    Includes index.
    Includes bibliographical references.
    ISBN 0-8018-4055-4 (alk. paper) — ISBN 0-8018-5118-1 (pbk. : alk. paper)
    1. Greek language—Rhetoric. 2. Greek literature—History and critcism—Theory, etc. 3. Greece—Intellectual life. 4. Rhetoric, Ancient. I. Title. II. Series.
PA401.C65 1991
808′.00938—dc200   90-36983 CIP

A catalog record for this book is available from the British Library.

Contents

Contents

Six
The Range and Limits of *Technē*   95

III: THE FOURTH CENTURY

Seven
Rhetoric and Prose   115

Eight
Rhetoric and Philosophy   139

Preface

The rhetoric of my title and of the investigation that follows is rhetoric in the narrowest and most conventional sense of the term: a speaker's or writer's self-conscious manipulation of his medium with a view to ensuring his message as favorable a reception as possible on the part of the particular audience being addressed. The self-consciously manipulative character of the process distinguishes rhetoric from eloquence, which may be unpremeditated and stem from nothing more than a natural knack for clear and expressive utterance; orientation toward a communicational goal distinguishes rhetoric from the type of verbal virtuosity in which the exploration or display of the resources of a given medium becomes an end in itself; indifference to the inherent character or value of the messages communicated so long as they are put across effectively distinguishes it from some of its modern namesakes—notably those which, in the wake of the twentieth-century "revival" of the subject, would make of rhetoric either an overall science of discourse or an art of practical reasoning and deliberation.

There is little if anything in this definition that would surprise the Greek founders of the discipline—or any of their successors, down to the early years of the nineteenth century. I argue, however, against the unanimous tradition derived from antiquity, that rhetoric so conceived and defined is neither the creation of a group of professors of public speech in the late fifth century, nor a system that emerged gradually out of attitudes toward speech and poetry well attested in Greece at a much earlier date. It is, rather, a typically fourth-century phenomenon, Plato and Aristotle being the earliest authors to recognize its existence or recommend (with certain restrictions) its use.

Greek literature before Plato is largely "arhetorical" in character: full of eloquence and argument but usually posited on the assumption of an essentially transparent verbal medium that neither impedes nor facilitates the transmission of information, emotions, and ideas. For the rhetorician's preoccupation with controlling the medium of transmission to come into play, two developments had to take place, neither of which would have occurred when it did without the contribution of Plato and Aristotle. First, audiences and composers had to acquire the habit of abstracting essential messages from verbal contexts: the informative core of any piece of communication from its non- or extra-informative—that is, rhetorical—residue. And such abstraction will only become widespread once essential messages can be formulated with the clarity and univalence which first became available to Greek discourse when the experimentation, uncertainty, and clash of contradictory ideologies that characterized fifth-century thought started to be replaced, largely through the work of Plato and Aristotle, by a stable, consistent body of what were widely regarded as universal truths. Second, a "written" eloquence had to come into being—that is, a body of prose texts which might be read or delivered verbatim and still suggest the excitement, atmosphere, and commitment of a spontaneous oral performance or debate. Plato—along with, to a lesser degree, the other Socratics and the orator Isocrates—was the first to compose such texts. Without such texts there would have been no satisfactory data base on which to conduct the detailed, precise analysis of the verbal medium that is characteristic of rhetoric.

The account of origins to which this book is dedicated seeks to trace the course and interaction of these two lines of development—toward the composing of written texts and toward the isolation of a composer's message from its verbal realization—up to the point where they became interwoven strands in the single fabric of mid-fourth-century rhetoric. It also seeks to show how and why the two lines of development came to be largely ignored in the traditional account, deriving ultimately from Plato and Aristotle themselves, according to which the fabric was already in existence in the late fifth century, but of poor quality, both morally and technically. While arguing for the superiority of my account to theirs, I have not sought to produce an *Aristotle's Criticism of the Pre-Platonic Rhetoricians,* however modest, to set beside the monumental studies of Harold Cherniss published by this press half a century ago. For that the available evidence is much too meager. The most one can hope to do is point to those pieces of evidence that indicate the lines a rewriting of the prehistory of rhetoric might have to take, were large portions of, say, Aristotle's *Synagōgē Technōn* available, and to invite the cooperation and criticism of other scholars in evaluating the material collected.

Cherniss's work has, of course, been an important influence on mine, simply by virtue of the possibilities that it forces any student of Aristotelian doxography to consider—as has the work of the late E. A. Havelock. Havelock encouraged one to look at rhetoric, as all other forms of Greek discourse, in the light of the complex evolution from oral to written forms of communication analyzed by him in a series of works published over the past twenty-five years. For specific criticisms and suggestions I am indebted to Glenn Most, Hayden Pelliccia, R. A. Prier, Vassily Rudich, and John Wallach, who read the book in typescript; to George Core and Bruno Gentili, who accepted portions of an earlier version of its argument for publication in *The Sewanee Review* and *Quaderni Urbinati;* to the two anonymous readers who served as referees for the Johns Hopkins University Press; and most of all, again, to Eric Havelock, for the many hours he devoted to help with the identification and clarification of problems—both in the rhetoric of the ancients and in my own.

Bibliographical Note

The standard works of reference and collections of fragments in the study of early Greek rhetoric are the following (abbreviated in citation as indicated):

A or B followed by an Arabic numeral = numbered "A" or "B" fragments in the section of H. Diels, *Fragmente der Vorsokratiker,* 7th ed. (Berlin, 1954), devoted to a given author. Section numbers are indicated, where necessary, by Arabic numerals immediately preceding A or B.

A or B followed by an Arabic numeral plus U = "A" or "B" fragments in the relevant section of M. Untersteiner, *Sofisti, Testimonianze e frammenti,* vols. 1–4 (Florence, 1949–67).

A or B followed by a Roman and then an Arabic numeral = fragments in L. Radermacher, *Artium scriptores* (Vienna, 1951).

Kennedy = G. Kennedy, *The Art of Persuasion in Ancient Greece* (Princeton, 1963).

Kroll = W. Kroll, "Rhetorik," *R-E* Suppl. 7 (Stuttgart, 1940), 1040–1138.

Lausberg = H. Lausberg, *Handbuch der literarischen Rhetorik* (Munich, 1960). References are to sections.

Volkmann = R. Volkmann, *Rhetorik der Griechen und Römer,* 3d ed. (Leipzig, 1901).

Fragments and other Greek texts are cited, wherever possible, in English translation (my own unless otherwise indicated). Citations of the works I have found most useful or relevant for specific points raised in the text may be found in the notes. Not cited there—because too much under the influence of the "official story" of rhetoric in the years 450 to 350 B.C.—are the three most elaborate discussions of pre-Platonic theory and its relation to early oratorical practice yet attempted:

P. Hamberger, *Die rednerische Disposition in der alten* τέχνη ῥητοριϰή = Rhetorische Studien 2 (Paderborn, 1914).

G. Kowalski, *De arte rhetorica*, vol. 1 (Lemberg, 1937).

O. Navarre, *Essai sur la rhétorique grecque avant Aristote* (Paris, 1900).

Readers who seek a more detailed corrective to the unconventionality of my own approach than can be found in either Kennedy or Kroll are referred to one of these works—preferably to the admirably clear and complete presentation offered by Navarre.

Also missing from the notes, because it appeared when the present work was already in press, is any reference to E. Schiappa's important article "Did Plato Coin *Rhētorikē?*" *AJP* 120 [1989]: 460-73.

The Origins of Rhetoric in Ancient Greece

One

Rhetoric, Neorhetoric, Protorhetoric

I t has been said that rhetoric is the will attempting to do the work of the imagination; and the earliest rhetoricians, Greeks of the fifth and fourth centuries B.C., might well have agreed. Only they would have put the matter rather differently, referring to the claims of "instruction" and "right reason" to replace "inspiration" or the favor of the Muse as a basis for preeminence in speech or song. It is equally possible and, as later chapters will argue, historically more accurate to define rhetoric as the written word attempting to do the work of the spoken word. All three formulations, however, envision the discipline in essentially the same way. Rhetoric is to poetry and eloquence what science is to magic, or philosophy to mythology, or politics and jurisprudence to the rule of ancestral tradition. It is the characteristic mode assumed by verbal skills in the wake of the intellectual revolution which, during the course of the sixth and fifth centuries B.C., laid the foundations for Western thought—and, as such, the natural successor to poetry and eloquence. Correspondingly, philosophy is the successor to mythology, science to magic, and politics to ancestral law. They are the characteristic "postrevolutionary" modes for the search into ultimate principles and causes, and for efforts to control and understand our physical or social environment.

1

This basic and, perhaps, quite obvious fact about rhetoric is too often obscured or ignored in standard accounts of its origin and development. The reason is twofold: first, the tendency, beginning in antiquity, to view the subject out of context, as a separate discipline with its own "founder," doxography, and canon of leading exponents; second, the practice, inaugurated by Plato and Aristotle, of using the word *rhetoric* to refer both to an essential part of their own pedagogical program and, rather more frequently, to the inept or irresponsible (so it seemed to them) anticipations and alternative versions of it to be found in the work of their contemporaries and predecessors. Rhetoric is thus made to seem, not only a discipline separated from philosophy, but one fundamentally at odds with it.

Yet it is in philosophical texts that we first hear of this discipline; and the word *rhetoric* itself bears every indication of being a Platonic invention. There is no trace of it in Greek before the point in the *Gorgias* (449a5) where the famous Sophist—after hesitation and (possibly) a certain amount of prompting from Socrates (448d9)—decides to call the art he teaches the "rhetorly"—that is, *rhētōr*'s or "speaker's"—"art" (*rhētorikē technē*). And the "speaker's art" would probably have sounded too much like the "shyster's" or "demagogue's art" for the historical Gorgias or any of his contemporaries to want to lay claim to it himself.[1] Even in the next generation the orator and educator Isocrates (c. 436–338 B.C.), usually credited with the creation of one of the two major "traditions" in ancient rhetorical theory, never uses the word—nor does any other Attic orator.[2] Down to the end of the fourth century, all occurrences are, with a single exception (p. 121), confined to Plato and Aristotle.

Whether and to what extent we are justified in using the term in dealing with non- or prephilosophical contexts is a question that subsequent chapters will attempt to answer. First, however, one must be clear about the character of the discipline as conceived by Plato and Aristotle themselves. For it fell to them, as completers, consolidators, and ultimately, principal beneficiaries of the sixth- and fifth-century revolution, to establish the basic categories and definitions that, here as everywhere, were to remain authoritative throughout antiquity and beyond.

The clearest and simplest of these authoritative pronouncements are definitions in terms of final cause. Rhetoric is the "artificer of persuasion" (Plato in the Gorgias [453a]) or the "influencing and swaying of the mind (psychagōgia) through words" (Plato in the Phaedrus [261a7–8]). More cautiously, it is the "capacity for seeing how to be as persuasive as subject and situation will permit" (Aristotle in the Rhetoric [1.2 1355b25–26], making allowance, as the medical analogy [1355b12–14] that accompanies his definition indicates, for a technically successful operation in which the rhetorician's client nevertheless dies). The conviction that persuasion produces may be true or false, but it ranks as belief, not knowledge—hence the Platonic distinction (Gorgias 454d–55a) between persuasion and teaching, and Aristotle's insistence (1.2 1356b34–57a7) that rhetoric is called for in situations where rigorous, conclusive demonstration is either unavailable, or incapable of being taken in by an audience.

Matters become more complicated once the two philosophers come to the discussion of means rather than ends. Here rhetoric is presented as a kind of hybrid, in that the procedures it uses are both like and unlike those employed by disciplines concerned with the attaining and transmitting of knowledge. Courtroom rhetoric is an imitation (Gorgias 463d2) of just dealing (dikaiosynē). It is related to the art of making and implementing just decisions in the same way as a gourmet cook's imitation of a nourishing menu is to the dietician's actual preparation of one, or a cosmetic imitation of physical beauty to the real beauty produced by athletic training. And this implies, given the nature of the analogies and the character of imitation itself as Plato conceives it, some sort of resemblance between model and copy. The appearance of justice (or nourishment or physical beauty) cannot be maintained unless there is some approximation, however imperfect, to the reality.

Aristotle is less consistent but more explicit about the nature of this approximation. He first defines rhetoric (Rhet. 1.1 1354a1) as a

3

counterpart to, or side growth on, the art of reasoning from plausible premises (dialectic in the Aristotelian understanding of the term), but then goes on to add an essential additional ingredient. Rhetoric is a compound discipline in which a dialectical component is supplemented by knowledge of how to arouse, or appeal to, an audience's emotions and impressions of a speaker's character (persuasion based on *ēthos* and *pathos* [1.2 1356a1–16], by contrast with the "rational" or *logos*-based persuasion supplied by dialectic). Aristotle is here echoing and developing Plato's view of rhetoric as a combination of understanding of one's subject matter and the ultimate issues and principles it exemplifies (dialectic, or a portion of it, in the Platonic understanding of the term: cf. *Phaedrus* 265c8–66c1) with knowledge of all the ways of talking about a thing (*logoi*) which will produce a desired reaction in a given audience under a given set of circumstances (*Phaedrus* 261a7–62c3 and 271c10–72a8).

Neither Plato nor Aristotle spells out in any detail the character of the relationship between the dialectical and nondialectical ingredients in the rhetorical mixture. Presumably it would vary with the situation, and no extended Platonic or Aristotelian analysis of such a situation survives. An elaborate dramatization of one does survive, however, in the form of the conversation recorded in the *Phaedrus;* and the three speeches on love found there receive a kind of commentary from the dramatic setting in which they appear. The commentary is largely implicit, but it is the closest either Plato or Aristotle ever comes to an extended piece of rhetorical exegesis—as well as the earliest such approach to be found anywhere in Greek.

Two of the speeches on love are delivered by Socrates in response to the third: a display piece, attributed to the orator Lysias, which Socrates' friend Phaedrus reads and extravagantly praises at the opening of the dialogue. Lysias's subject is the disaster likely to befall a boy or youth when he has an affair with an older man passionately in love with him. Better take up with someone who does not love you than with someone who does is the advice Lysias has for the young, paradoxically presented in the form of a courtship speech delivered to a boy by a self-proclaimed "nonlover." In it the speaker seeks to advance his own suit by pointing out that shared interests and mutual respect are a securer basis for a liaison than physical passion felt by only one of the two parties. The argument is sensible enough once divested of its paradoxical trappings, but its prosaic, utilitarian practicality is anathema to Socrates.[3] He counters with what turns out to be a pair of closely integrated speeches designed to win Phaedrus over—or back—to Platonic eros. The core of this counterargument is a dialectical definition, carried out in accordance with the method of collection and division illustrated at length in the *Sophist* and the *Politicus*. Socrates defines love by first locating it correctly in the general category of frenzies or madnesses affecting the soul, then revealing its exact position within this category through a series of subdivisions. The result is a distinction between two types of love, one of which belongs alongside gluttony and dipsomania as a form of irrational and uncontrolled drive for physical satisfaction, the other with the gift of prophecy or poetry as a heaven-sent madness that benefits its recipient. Amorous madness of the latter sort is the desperate longing that the sight of human beauty arouses in the soul. Though imperfect, human beauty reminds the soul of that absolute beauty which it apprehended directly at a prior stage of its existence, unmediated by the physical senses and outside the spatiotemporal realm to which the senses are confined. Beauty's image thus beheld in the beloved, along with the beloved's contemplation of the reflection kindled by the beloved's own beauty in the soul of the lover, can result in a joint effort to recapture more fully the vision of beauty both souls once enjoyed, and this leads in its turn to a more perfect ordering of two lives in accordance with the memory of all the celestial or supercelestial forms once glimpsed alongside that of beauty. Such love, provided the baser desires for physical union that accompany it are suppressed or minimized, is a source of far greater good than anything stemming from the "earth-bound caution and restraint" (*sōphrosynē thnētē*: 256e5) which would make a youth prefer the attentions of a nonlover to those of a lover.

Such is the "dialectical" component of Socrates' defense, here presented, as Plato presents it later in the dialogue (265e1–66a8),

5

in straightforward summary form. He does not present it this way at the outset, however, and the oblique, piecemeal, and at times misleading procedures which Socrates uses instead are a fair indication of the sort of thing that must be joined to dialectic to produce rhetoric.

Socrates takes up the case at the point where his client Love is the victim of what ancient rhetoricians call *diabolē*: the unfavorable prejudice created by circumstances preceding the trial.[4] The regular remedy in such a situation is the inclusion of a section early on in the defense, which complains of this fact and digresses—often with apologies for delaying the business at hand—into what is, strictly speaking, an irrelevant examination of the past. In the *Apology* Plato has Socrates make just such a digression before he replies to the charges of Meletus. Here the technique is similar, but more subtle. Initially, the only objection of substance Socrates makes to Lysias's charges has to do with their obviousness (235e5–36a2): it is the ostentatious and repetitive character of their style that disturbs him more than anything else (235a1–8), and he thinks he must have heard better things along the same line elsewhere (235c1–d3). This procedure is effective in two ways. It avoids a head-on confrontation with the enthusiasm inspired by Lysias's criticism of love; at the same time the remark about other treatments of its theme has the effect—doubtless intentional—of provoking the word-intoxicated Phaedrus into demanding that Socrates reproduce what he has heard. The defense of love is thus launched at Phaedrus's insistence rather than Socrates', and by what seems at first an attack centered around the same general point that Lysias had made. Socrates, as he himself implies in 237b1–6, is in the position of a crafty lover advancing Love's cause and his own by pretending not to be in love with the boy he is courting.

The "attack" begins by defining the bad sort of love in isolation, as if there were no other type to be considered, and then proceeds to catalogue its disastrous consequences—spiritual, bodily, and material—with the methodical thoroughness such a down-to-earth position demands. All this is susceptible to misinterpretation, but it caters to Phaedrus's present determination to hear nothing good of love, while at the same time refraining from anything that cannot be made to point to a very different conclusion later—once Socrates has revealed the full nature of the matter under discussion. The only thing that might be incompatible with such a conclusion would be extended praise of the nonlover, of which there had been a good deal in Lysias. This Socrates avoids for the time being with a typical rhetorical *brachylogia*: to Phaedrus's complaint, upon completion of the first speech, that half of its argument still remains to be presented, he replies (241e5–6) that the nonlover's virtues are simply the reverse of all the lover's faults and so need not be enumerated.

When the time finally comes to reveal the inadequacy of his initial approach, Socrates is able to capitalize on this desire for a companion speech of contrasting character, merely substituting the bad lover–good lover contrast for the expected one between lover and nonlover. But as a further means of ensuring a good reception, he avails himself of the advice of those (cf. Arist., *Rhet.* 3.17 1418b24–33) who recommend cushioning the effect of a potentially disturbing remark by making someone else responsible for it. His handling of the case would have been over, he claims, but for an admonitory sign from his *daimonion*— a sure indication that Love demands a recantation of the insult which His divinity has just sustained (242b8–c3). The ensuing praise of Love thus owes its position in the defense—and the very fact that it comes in the form of a palinode—to the rhetorical demands of the situation.

The contents of the second speech are just as much a response to rhetorical considerations as its location and form. Here the determining factor is the character of the audience: Phaedrus's sincere if somewhat superficial enthusiasm for things philosophical, and his rather deeper enthusiasm for beauty, whether found in Greek prose or Greek boys. Explicit dialectic is accordingly avoided for the most part—even though defining the good form of love involves a number of contentions that could have been so argued had Socrates chosen: the composite character of the soul (deduced in the *Republic* [4.434d–41c] from the inability of any noncompound entity to be affected in contradictory ways by the same stimulus at the same time); the soul's access, at some "non-human" phase of its existence, to knowledge of a purely noetic realm of being (inferred at *Meno* 80e–86b from one's apparent ability to perceive the truth of mathematical propositions concerning which one has had no prior instruction), and the immortality of the soul (a corollary to its definition as the self-moving [cf. *Laws* 10.892a–99d]).

Socrates begins by arguing the last of these points very briefly (245c–e), in a passage designed to impress as much by the hieratic solemnity of its language as the rigor of its dialectic. The rest appears, along with a good deal of material not essential for the argument, in the brilliant and alluring guise of a "mythic hymn" (cf. 265c1): the winged charioteer and team of horses, one noble and one base, that is the soul (245e–46d); the soul's periodic effort, in its disembodied state, to rise beyond the top of the firmament to feast its wings on the forms of the real (246d–47e); the base horse's inability to respond to the commands of its charioteer, the loss of the soul's wings through undernourishment and its ensuing fall from the zenith (248a–49d); finally, the half ecstatic, half painful sprouting of new wings once, in embodied form, the soul is roused to memory of what it once perceived through the sight of beauty's reflection in a beautiful boy (250c–53c). All this is likeness at best, and much of the imagery is not intended to bear close scrutiny once the trappings of myth are stripped away. (Cf. Socrates' own evaluation at 265b6–8.) There is no passage of comparable length and brilliance whose total excision from the Platonic corpus would be of less consequence for our understanding of Platonic philosophy.

Equally striking is the absence of any detailed account of the lover's upward progress from infatuation with embodied beauty to contemplation of beauty itself that looms so large in the Platonic passage that most closely resembles this one, Diotima's speech in the *Symposium*. There, however, the audience addressed is the philosopher Socrates. Here it is the philosophical pederast Phaedrus (cf. 249a1); and Phaedrus is not required to imagine lover and lad as achieving anything more than common devotion to the particular god under whose patronage their souls made the original ascent to feast on what lies beyond the firmament. The reader of the dialogue may be intended to realize that there is something higher to which a soul can aspire, even in its embodied state; and to wonder how desperate longing for this higher thing comes to be replaced by fixation on a single individual. But Phaedrus is not encouraged to do so.[5]

Owing in no small part to such expert limitations on its content, the speech is a complete success—and, to judge from the durability of the entire tradition of Platonic love that goes back to this dialogue, a success with Phaedrus's spiritual descendants as well as with Phaedrus himself. It is as accomplished and effective a piece of continuous rhetoric as survives from antiquity, rivaled only by certain speeches of Demosthenes and Cicero, sections of Plato's own *Gorgias* and *Phaedo,* and, of course, the whole of his *Apology.* The last can be counted a rhetorical failure only on the mistaken assumption that its passionate, unyielding defense of Socrates' philosophical mission is directed at an actual Athenian jury, rather than at the audience of literate intellectuals, unsuited by taste or talent for an active political life and the compromises it requires, for whom Plato was in fact writing.

The argument that Socrates shapes, distorts, expands, compresses, ornaments stylistically, or modifies in other ways to ensure optimum reception by a particular audience in a particular situation is evidently regarded by Plato as a valid one—or as valid a one as Phaedrus is able to understand and profit from. And since Plato sees dialectic as the philosopher's supreme means of discovering the true nature of reality, it follows that the dialectically accomplished rhetorician has absolute mastery both of the facts of any case he pleads and all that can be correctly inferred from them. He has, however, a certain leeway in the use he makes of this knowledge. The more thorough and exact a speaker's understanding of the ways things are, the greater his ability to capitalize on those resemblances which allow an audience to be deceived into mistaking one thing for another (*Phaedrus* 261e6–62d6). Thus it is Socrates' dialectically grounded awareness of the way the two types of love resemble each other as different manifestations of soul-possessing madness that allows him to present a part of love as if it were the whole in his initial discussion of the subject.

Here, as elsewhere in Plato (*Hipp. Min.* 366e–67a5), a thorough knowledge of the truth produces the most reluctant liars, but also the most successful ones. Speakers whose knowledge is not complete—not inclusive, for example, of the subject of discourse but only of the character of a particular audience and the methods of argumentation likely to be most effective with it—will accordingly be incomplete rhetoricians. But this is because their ignorance makes them less versatile and effective, not because the perfect rhetorician is always committed to telling the truth.

The dialectical demands that true rhetoric must meet are much less stringent in Aristotle than in Plato—a reflection of the change Aristotle has introduced in the notion of dialectic itself. The discipline is no longer the ultimate method for arriving at philosophical truth that it was in Plato; it is, rather, the art of coming up with and arguing from premises of the sort an opponent is likely to accept in a dialectical debate.[6]

The rhetoric that is a counterpart to this, or compounded out of it and some other set of skills, requires a corresponding ability to produce the premises and inferences a deliberative or judicial body is likely to accept (*Rhet.* 1.2 1356b35–57a1). And insofar as it is provided by Aristotle's great treatise, the rhetorician's training in dialectic or a counterpart to dialectic involves mastering, first, an inventory of truths, partial truths, and received truths of the sort likely to provide acceptable premises for argument, and then another inventory (much less extensive than that required of the dialectician) of the logical operations by which further truths can be derived, or made to seem to derive, from those premises. The premises, drawn from the realms of ethics, politics, jurisprudence, and criminology, and arranged according to the type of oratory (forensic, deliberative, or epideictic) most likely to make use of them, constitute the bulk of Book 1 of the *Rhetoric,* whereas the inventory of logical operations closes Book 2.

The methodology becomes somewhat more complicated in the intervening chapters, where Aristotle passes from the strictly dialectical aspects of his subject (*logos*) to a discussion of proofs based on *ēthos* and *pathos.* In addition to the true or generally accepted ideas of the way people behave and should behave that can be used arguing a point dialectically, there are many others which can be used indirectly as well—not to establish a point but because giving voice to them produces a certain impression of a speaker's character (*ēthos*), or fits in with or inspires certain audience emotions (*pathos*). Still others need not be mentioned at all but provide the speaker with a basis for the reasoning that leads him to select those premises he does decide to mention.[7]

It is to the second and third types of speaker's premise—largely psychological in character—that the second book of the *Rhetoric* is principally devoted: a series of generalizations about the attitudes of certain groups of people (the old, the young, the rich, the poor, etc.) or of general formulations having to do with the kind of audience emotions a speaker is likely to encounter, the type of person likely to feel them, and the situation or person likely to provoke them.

The rest of Aristotle's treatment of the nondialectical aspect of his subject deals with style and arrangement (Book 3). It is even more specifically rhetorical than the discussion found in Book 2, in that the entire justification for its presence is its relevance to the task of affecting a given audience in a given way.

This sharp isolation of style and arrangement as a subject for independent treatment is probably an Aristotelian innovation. Both skills are amply illustrated by Socratic example in the *Phaedrus*, but Plato has no special rubric for them when he comes to speak explicitly of the prerequisites for successful practice of the art. They would evidently be regarded as ingredients in the various *logoi* that the rhetorician must have at his disposal if he is to put across what dialectic teaches him; and the category of *logoi* embraces much that Aristotle would classify as argumentation. But Aristotle's different procedure makes sense as part of a consistent effort to develop some workable means of realizing the rhetorical program laid down by Plato—a program calling for knowledge of all the relevant facts and principles involved in a given case and all the potentially useful ways of presenting them as well. Aristotle abandons the demand for universal mastery of all conceivable techniques and subject matter in favor of a concentration on certain recurring items (premises in Book 1, pointers on style and

11

arrangement in Book 3 which can be isolated and enumerated; and psychology as a whole gives way to the specific emotions (anger, fear, pity, indignation, envy, etc.) and the specific groups (old, young, rich, poor, etc.) to which orators most often appeal. Narrowed range and increased specificity and practicality do not, however, prevent the discipline set forth at length in the *Rhetoric* from being essentially the same one envisioned in the *Phaedrus*. And taken together, the two works provide the set of underlying, often unacknowledged, assumptions about the nature of discourse that were destined to provide the foundations for rhetoric as taught and practiced throughout the rest of antiquity, the Middle Ages, and well into modern times.

The most important of these assumptions is the absolute separability of a speaker's message from the method used to transmit it.[8] Translated into the language of later handbooks, this assumption produces the need for separate chapters devoted to resourcefulness in coming up with arguments (*heuresis, inventio*) on the one hand and, on the other, skill in their arrangement (*diathesis, dispositio*), stylistic presentation (*lexis, elocutio*), and delivery (*hypokrisis, actio*). At the same time, on the method side of the dichotomy, it is assumed that there exist a number of equally available and, so far as the message itself is concerned, equally adequate means of transmission—those, for example, determined by the particular selection which, on any given occasion, a speaker working in the Platonic-Aristotelian tradition makes from among the various premises, *logoi,* logical operations, and stylistic techniques he has mastered. At least one of these means of transmission will be "nonrhetorical" in that it does not employ any of the audience- or situation-directed techniques that are the specific property of the rhetorician. It is the message and nothing more: a story plainly told, without *ēthos* or *pathos*, or a point dialectically supported as directly, efficiently, and unambiguously as possible. The rest are all "rhetorical" in that they enclose the basic message in a verbal context that says more or less or other than what the speaker means, but always in such a way that the message is better received for having to be extracted or supplied rather than taken in directly.

It may, for example, be more easily understood because of such things as examples, summaries, repetitions, and the relief provided by humor and digressions; or more readily assented to because it uses the kind of argument with which the audience is most familiar or the premises it finds most congenial and flattering; or more eagerly acted upon because the speaker moves his hearers even while his ostensible aim is simply to convince.

This distinction between rhetorical and nonrhetorical means of presentation may well seem to us an unreal (or unrealistic) one, but it is also a crucial one—a telling indication of the degree to which the whole discipline is defined, as a philosopher might be expected to define it, in residual, negative terms. Rhetoric is that part of any self-consciously calculated piece of communication which fails to meet a philosopher's standards of accuracy, coherence, and consistency, but is still necessary if the communication is to be fully successful. Rhetorical discourse is not the opposite of philosophical discourse but rather, in most situations, its complementary contrary, and only capable of being identified and studied by reference to the appropriate philosophical counterpart.

The distinction between philosophical core and aphilosophical residue that is fundamental to the rhetorical conception of argumentation is equally important for the rhetorical doctrine of composition and arrangement. Here the place of dialectical argumentation is taken by logical and chronological ordering of events and ideas, or by "normal" word order.[9] Anything else is some sort of deviation and, as such, a means of attracting attention and so coloring the basic message in various ways. It can, for example, create a formal unity that underlines—or tries to compensate for the lack of—thematic unity; or it can isolate and highlight the items to which an audience is likely to be the most receptive, thereby influencing the way an entire presentation is received.

On the level of style, what corresponds to dialectic or straightforward narrative is the norm of plain, idiomatic speech moving always at the level of strict, univocal literalness, from which the figurative language taught by the rhetorician is a deviation. Some theoreticians in antiquity questioned whether a truly "unfigured" discourse is possible, but their position was evidently a minority

13

one, now attested in a single text (Alexander Numeniu, *De figuris* pp. 12 ff. Spengel).[10] Elsewhere Aristotle's notion (*Rhet.* 3.2 1404b1 ff.) of effective style as the result of a series of calculated deviations from the everyday forms the ultimate basis for the whole study of figures and tropes, even though no agreement on the why of this effectiveness was ever reached. The meaning transmitted in "deviant" fashion may be experienced as more impressive because of the general poetic associations that cling to figurative language, or more acceptable because of the attractiveness that the newness and strangeness of the figure possesses, or more memorable because the hearer has had to work to grasp it, or more to the hearer's liking because he has in effect supplied his own idea of what the speaker ought to mean in the process of interpreting a context that is deliberately overstated, understated, or otherwise imprecise. And these, of course, are only a few of the possibilities.

At whatever level rhetoric operates, however, its aim must be to secure in some fashion or another a better reception for the speaker's message. Saying something other than what one means is not rhetorical when it merely seeks to conceal meaning from one possible audience (the uneducated, for example, or the uninitiated, or the wielders of political censorship) without any corresponding enhancement in the way meaning is received by the audience for whom it is intended. Nor is the simple conveying of a message known to be false (lying) or an argument known to be fallacious (sophistry) rhetorical per se, however often rhetoric may be used to make lies seem like truth or introduce sophistry in such a way that its fallaciousness passes unnoticed. For pure lies and sophistry to succeed, the audience must remain completely unaware of what is going on. Successful rhetoric, on the other hand, presupposes a certain level of audience sophistication. It fails altogether if the hearer takes in only the literal meaning of a word used figuratively, or cannot distinguish basic argument from illustrative example, or does not recognize that the hysteron in a hysteron-proteron is really proteron and vice versa. Rhetoric's presence is always clear at some level to the audience; it is only the why of its presence that is not.

The speaker, of course, is fully aware of the why of everything he says, and his conscious manipulation of the transmission of meaning at all levels distinguishes the art (rhetoric) he possesses from the mere power or ability (eloquence) of a naturally effective speaker. Rhetorical performance always presupposes a certain amount of rhetorical theory and analysis—hence the use of the terms *rhetoric* and *rhetorician* to refer both to study and practice, critic and performer. Eloquence does not presuppose such study, nor on the other hand does the study and practice of rhetoric necessarily result in what is usually thought of as eloquence. Certain kinds of plain speech or purely dialectical argumentation can qualify as rhetoric if their use stems from the calculated conviction that in the situation at hand it is more effective than any other available means of presentation. Typical instances are the bare narrative of the "facts" of the case often found in ancient oratory, or the rhetorical "sublime" as usually conceived: "a style in which figure is strictly absent . . . a *zero degree* . . . the value of which ["absolute sobriety of expression" being "the mark of extreme elevation in thought"] is perfectly recognized."[11] Such transmissions are a kind of minimal rhetoric. Only the speaker's end is rhetorical; the means he deploys are borrowed from other verbal modes or are the common property of all modes.

The process of borrowing can, of course, proceed in the opposite direction, resulting in the introduction of specifically rhetorical procedures into other verbal arts. References to drama, epigram, epic, and lyric are found in both Plato's *Phaedrus* and Aristotle's *Rhetoric,* and Plato explicitly includes poetic and legal discourse along with oratory in the comparison of the value of the written and oral word with which his dialogue closes (278b7–d1). Aristotle's rigid use of the categories forensic, symbouleutic, and epideictic makes the explicit focus of the *Rhetoric* much narrower, but its sister treatise the *Poetics* and the later works influenced by it are a striking testimony to the pervasiveness of his rhetorical categories and assumptions. Their presence in the *Poetics* has often been noted,[12] but there is still a tendency to underestimate their importance.

Corresponding to Aristotle's notion of dialectical argument as the main body (*sōma*) of rhetorical persuasion (*Rhet.* 1.1 1354a14–

15

15) is his view that the "soul," as it were, of tragedy resides in its basic narrative argument or plot (*mythos* [*Poetics* 6.1450a37–38]). Both types of argument, dialectical and narrative, are separable from the rest of the play or speech. Aristotle even suggests (17 1455a34–b15) that plot—in its most abstract and general form—be in fact so separated in the poet's mind prior to being particularized in time and place and embodied in a series of episodes. The remaining, less essential parts of the dramatist's art would presumably be brought into play at an even later stage in the process: fleshing out plot structure with the expression of sentiments (*dianoia*) and the revelation of character (*ēthos*) that monologue and dialogue contain, and overlaying the whole with the sweetenings of style, melody, and spectacle (*lexis, melos, opsis*) in such a way to ensure its reception with appropriate feelings of pleasure, pity, and fear. These feelings are doubtless more intense, but not different in kind from those that a bare presentation of the particular narrative argument of a play would produce. It is enough to hear of what happened to Oedipus to experience pity and fear (14 1453b3–7); one does not have to attend a performance of Sophocles.

Verisimilitude of plot and argument is essential to the success of both orator and dramatist, even if to different degrees and in somewhat different ways. Both can find themselves committed to making a given version of events seem as likely as possible. This is always the poet's task: whether the subject matter is original or taken from history and legend, it must be presented not simply as something that has happened but as the *sort* of thing that *might* happen (9 1451a37–38). And it is the orator's task whenever, as frequently occurs, there is not enough evidence to establish his case through a series of compelling inferences and he must settle for plausible reconstruction of past events. Each is denied certain procedures available to the other. The poet does not have the orator's ability to convey information and rouse emotions via direct authorial pronouncement. When the action of the play itself fails to perform these functions he must operate indirectly, through the commentary (*didaskalia*) contained in the *dianoia* of his characters (cf. 19 1456b2–6). On the other hand the poet has the advantage—at least if his plot comes from history or legend—that the audience knows or believes the events on which it is based to have taken place (what has in fact happened once is also thought to be the *sort* of thing that happens: 9 1451b15–19).

The formal differences between such poetic imitations and oratorical *narratio* are minimized by Aristotle's decision, first, to expand Plato's use of the term *mimesis* to include narrative as well as dramatic presentations (contrast *Rep.* 3.392c ff. with *Poetics* 3 1448a19–24); and, second, to argue that the element of spectacle is not essential to drama, since the force (*dynamis*) of tragedy is the same in both reading and performance (*Poetics* 6 1450b18–19). Poet and orator thus become workers in essentially the same purely verbal medium; and they are under similar constraints: not to choose a story which is incapable of providing the basis for a plausible *mythos* in the one instance (*Poetics* 24 1460a33–34), not to take up a hopeless case in the other; and (in both instances) not to make the mistake of preferring implausible truth to plausible falsehood. The license for extravagant language and improbable episodes that traditionally distinguished poet from orator is largely ignored by Aristotle, or mentioned only to minimize its significance. It is part of the pathology of style, something conceded to poets as a pardonable fault (25 1460b11–13) when it cannot be explained away (ch. 25 passim); but it must—like the quest for monstrous and outlandish stage effects (15 1453b8–11)—be condemned outright if it leads to what is obscure and unidiomatic (22 1458a23–30).

Aristotle's famous contention (9 1451b6–8) that poetry, by virtue of its favoring of the general over the particular, is more "philosophical" than history is often interpreted as a further indication of the degree to which a rhetorical approach permeates the *Poetics*. Plot itself, in this view, is a kind of rhetorical exemplum, a means of illustrating, through some particular series of events, a general truth about the way men and women behave or ought to behave. Aristotle himself need not have gone quite so far as this interpretation suggests: he could, for example, have seen poetry's preoccupation with the general as simply an incidental consequence of its mimetic character. To be recognized as a good imitation—and so cause the pleasure such recognition brings (cf. 4

1448b15–19)—poetry must deal with things concerning which all members of an audience have shared similar impressions; and such things usually involve life in general as it is, or ought to be, lived—not particular events or persons that happen to be fixed in everyone's memory in the same way.[13] But if the notion of literary subject matter as illustrative exemplum goes beyond Aristotle, it goes beyond him along a path in fact taken by his successors,[14] and in a direction in which he himself had made the decisive move through his notion of the mimetically successful plot as the *sine qua non* of tragedy.

More or less the same applies to the other divergences that can be pointed out between rhetoric as envisaged by Plato and Aristotle and as envisaged or practiced by their successors. Tendencies already present in the fourth century are intensified, or appear in connection with a wider range of phenomena. Plato's general category of *logoi* suited to prevailing upon a given audience at a given time was subdivided by Aristotle into the "ethical" and "pathetical" premises of Book 2 of the *Rhetoric* and the modes of arrangement and diction of Book 3. This division still recognizes the existence of special argumentative procedures dictated by occasion and audience rather than subject matter, and so of a kind of bridge between the dialectical component of rhetoric with which the treatise begins and the narrowly stylistic concerns with which it closes.

The bridge tends to disappear in later writers, as the number of basic ingredients in rhetorical expertise is reduced in one fashion or another to two. A single basic task, the finding or devising of arguments (*heuresis/inventio*) is set in sharp contrast to another (arrangement and diction, diction and its attending figures of speech, now being seen as the principal source of an orator's powers to make a message more impressive and moving).[15] The basic opposition becomes more pronounced and symmetrical because of a further tendency to replace the arrangement–diction pair with a single entity that acts as an exact counterpart to the single category of *inventio*. Sometimes diction is neglected and arrangement alone considered (as in the discussion of rules for composition in different types of genres discussed by the late author known as Menander Rhetor). At other times arrangement is relegated to the status of addendum to *inventio*, a simple indication of what section of a speech—prologue, narrative, proof, epilogue— is most appropriate for a given argument. This classification under- lies the method of organization found in the principal Latin au- thorities on rhetoric: the Auctor ad Herennium and, to a lesser degree, Cicero and Quintilian. Alternatively, both diction and ar- rangement may be placed under one rubric (Hermagoras's *oiko- nomia*, for example).

When, as often occurs in later antiquity, the study of diction becomes the major focus of the rhetorician's attention, the matter– method dichotomy has simply been—for understandable rea- sons—partially submerged, not eliminated altogether. With rhet- oric recognized as the all-embracing category to which every type of artistic discourse belongs, *inventio* is a subject too broad for the competence of any single person. Rhetoricians are accordingly expected to borrow the content of what they say more or less intact from other disciplines: philosophy, jurisprudence, ethics, and poli- tics, or, in the case of literary elaboration of a given theme, history, biography, and even science. To these add theology, once *ars rheto- rica* acquires, as a main subdivision, the medieval *ars praedicandi*.

Ancient rhetoric's two fundamental assumptions—separability of matter from method and the existence of a number of equally adequate methods for transmitting any given piece of subject mat- ter—are also assumptions whose rejection has been a fundamental factor in the decline of the discipline in the past two centuries. The second notion is incompatible with the widely held romantic or "expressionist" notion of the literary work as a unique or max- imally adequate verbalization of a unique vision or unique individ- ual sensibility. To think of such a production in rhetorical terms is as inconceivable as expecting a new version of it whenever the author gives a public reading before a new audience. The first notion is incompatible with the central position that close reading and interpretation of texts has come to occupy in literary studies. If an author's meaning is a subject of discussion only to the extent that it is concretized through the sentences and paragraphs of a particular document, the rhetorician's outlines and paraphrases become almost an impertinence. And either notion is, at best, irrelevant to the formalist or structuralist effort to study literary technique, so far as possible, without reference to the individual creator's intention and choice of subject matter. The same applies *a fortiori* to the deconstructionist or reader-response critic's concentration on intentionality and selectivity as part of the process of literary reception rather than literary genesis.

The antirhetorical character of our age is nowhere more evident than in the failure of various twentieth-century attempts to revive the discipline through the resurrection of selected ancient categories and pieces of terminology. However valuable the resulting specimens of "neorhetoric" may be in themselves, the resemblance they bear to their ancient namesake is fairly superficial. The discipline is aggrandized virtually beyond recognition in the work of those neorhetoricians—Kenneth Burke and Ch. Perelmann, for example—who wish to turn it into an art of practical reasoning concerned not simply with mastering, as need arises, premises drawn from ethics, politics, psychology, or wherever, but making significant additions on its own to the total store of such wisdom.[16] To proceed in this fashion is, as Aristotle says (*Rhet.* 1.4 1359b12), to claim for rhetoric what belongs to a different art; and later antiquity, with the exception of Cicero and Quintilian in their more assertive moments, would have agreed. Plato's contemporary Isocrates does make such claims for the discipline *he* teaches and practices—but the Isocratean word for that discipline is regularly *philosophia,* never *rhētorikē.*

One finds the boundaries of the province of rhetoric laid down more or less as they were in antiquity, but its basic character and methodology fundamentally transformed, in those modern works devoted to the literary techniques and strategies that constitute what is now called the "rhetoric" of a particular genre.[17] Here style and method of presentation are seen, in rhetorical fashion, as means deployed toward a given communicative end, but there is little trace of the rhetorician's tendency to view these means as subject to variation whose aim is not a deeper, subtler coming to terms with the author's meaning but merely

What oft was thought but ne'er so well expressed.

Pope's formula covers a basic goal of rhetoric ubiquitously encountered (though never so well expressed). It inspires everything from the ancient schoolboy's earliest prescribed efforts to retell in his own words the argument of a poem to the mature literary artist's reworking of topics and *topoi* sanctioned by literary precedent. But it is also a goal basically foreign to neorhetoric.[18] The study of "rhetorical" techniques and strategies as now conducted is far more likely to involve an adaptation of ancient terminology to the expressionist notion of the uniquely adequate verbalization of a unique idea.

Expanded in scope or transformed in character in the two adaptations just considered, the discipline undergoes what is in effect a complete inversion when neorhetoricians discuss the nature and workings of figurative language.[19] Although the point of departure here is the ancient catalogue of tropes and figures, its contents are now studied with an eye on the multiplication rather than—as in antiquity—the reduction of meaning in any given piece of artistic discourse. Classical rhetoric is inconceivable apart from dialectic, and continues, once it has been conceived and defined, to require the orientation that dialectic and plain speech provide. They are an unmediated expression of meaning, reference to which helps the rhetorician keep in mind the basic import of those contexts in which the medium has been made intentionally opaque through a speaker's preoccupation with the added emphases and nuances, shaping and distortions that will ensure optimum reception for his message. For the neorhetorician, on the other hand, such "additions" are as fundamental a part of a piece of communication as any other. Dialectic and plain speech count as atypical phenomena, the result of a conscious effort to construct contexts in which the natural vagueness and multivalence of verbal signifiers is kept at a minimum. Figurative language—at least when the figures used are original ones—allows this natural multivalence full play:

> The operation of discourse set in motion by metaphor is just the inverse
> of that which we have just described [making "sense" through the

21

elimination of ambiguity]. For a sentence to make sense . . . it is necessary . . . that all the acceptations of the semantic potential of the word
under consideration be eliminated *except one,* that which is compatible
with the meaning, itself appropriately reduced, of the other words of
the sentence. In the case of metaphor, none of the already codified
acceptations is suitable; it is necessary, therefore, to retain all the acceptations allowed *plus one,* that which will rescue the meaning of the
entire statement.[20]

Thus does the neorhetorician's single text with many meanings
take the place of the rhetorician's single meaning with many texts.

Virtually the only areas where rhetoric is still vigorously practiced
are those of propaganda and advertising, and the low esteem in
which those arts are generally held, even by their practitioners, is yet
another testimony to the antirhetorical character of our times.

The age of anti- and neorhetoric is rather less than two centuries
old, and the developments that led to it can still be studied in some
detail—as one aspect of the larger passage from classical to romantic in Western thought and culture.[21] The developments that led to
the rather more than two millennia (roughly 400 B.C.–A.D. 1800)
of the age of rhetoric are much more obscure. Already for Plato and
Aristotle, rhetoric meant very much what it was to mean throughout these two millennia; but it is very difficult to say just how their
understanding of the term arose, whether by an act of creation *ex
nihilo* to suit their own purposes, or through radical transformation
of earlier ideas about effective speech, or in the course of appropri-
ation, with minor modifications, of ideas already current but not
linked to the term *rhētorikē.*

In electing, as they do by and large, for the third of these
possibilities, classical scholars have been guided partly by the
testimony from later antiquity that ascribes rhetorical treatises and
specific rhetorical precepts to a number of "protorhetoricians" in
the two generations before Plato's (Corax and Tisias at Syracuse in
the mid-fifth century; Gorgias, Thrasymachus, Polus, Theodorus,
and others at Athens and elsewhere in the decades of the Peloponnesian War). But they are also influenced by the feeling—a hold-

over from the age of rhetoric itself—that something as natural and inevitable as the rhetorical conception of the nature of effective speech could never have lain too far below the surface of the Greek consciousness. Explicit formulation of a body of useful precepts could be expected to follow, by a process of easy, gradual evolution, once there arose—as there did in Athens and Syracuse in the second quarter of the fifth century—democratic political regimens in which eloquence might well count for more in the pursuit of fame and power than wealth and family.

The ancient testimony on which this reconstruction rests is inconsistent, however—both with itself and with the modern "evolutionary" model that has been imposed upon it. Corax and Tisias, the supposed cofounders of the whole tradition, are often credited with a fairly impressive set of achievements: nothing less than the isolation (for the first time in antiquity) of oratorical form and structure as a suitable subject for investigation, the identification and description (also for the first time) of a number of typical argumentational and stylistic procedures, and a prescriptive analysis—destined to remain canonical throughout antiquity—of the use and positioning of these procedures within one particular formal structure, that of the judicial oration. It is hard to reconcile this initial burst of creative activity with the usual Platonic and Aristotelian picture (*Phaedr.* 266d1–69c5, *Rhet.* 1.1 1354a11–16, 1354b16–19, and 3.13 1414a36–b18) of protorhetoric as a collection of trivialities. And either picture is hard to reconcile with Aristotle's account (in one atypical passage [*Soph. El.* 33.183b29–84b3]) of how first Tisias, then Thrasymachus, Theodorus, and others, through a series of individually insignificant contributions, gradually created the foundations for a true art of rhetoric—much superior, in this respect, to what was created by the first masters in the practice of dialectic.

A possible reconciliation, taking into account the overall outlines of what is now generally believed about protorhetoric, might go somewhat as follows: Tisias and Corax, we may assume, supplied merely the basic idea and format for subsequent handbooks, a format enlarged but not essentially altered as members of the next generation recognized the existence of further subdivisions in the structure of the judicial oration and produced vastly expanded catalogues of appropriate figures of speech and modes of argument. These will have been the piecemeal additions of which Aristotle speaks, additions that resulted ultimately in a whole more impressive than any of its parts. Presumably, however, the accretions were almost purely quantitative in character. Though we are informed of sporadic efforts to give separate treatment to new topics such as delivery and nonjudicial oratory, real qualitative progress must have come only in the third and fourth generation, when Plato and Aristotle decided to turn the focus of the discipline from manner to matter, insisting that a proper understanding of the content and purpose of all public discourse (political and ceremonial as well as judicial) must precede instruction in oratorical method. It is overall dissatisfaction with protorhetoric's self-imposed limitations that explains the judgment found in Plato— and in Aristotle as well, outside the passage just mentioned. Aristotle shared Plato's dissatisfaction, but was capable, on one occasion, at least, of seeing and judging the proponents of the discipline in their own terms.

Even when assessed on their own terms, however, the *relative* achievements of inaugurators and continuers as reported elsewhere are difficult to square with this judgment of Aristotle in the way the reconstruction just offered suggests. One wonders whether skeptics (such as Kroll) are not right in rejecting the whole tradition about the content of Corax's handbook (cf. Kroll 1046). This tradition is first attested in the sixth century A.D. and may well be a late fabrication—the result of the well-documented ancient tendency to assume that the main outlines of any intellectual discipline are already to be found *in nucleo* in the work of its founder. This assumption will have allowed the four canonical parts of the judicial oration and the separate persuasive functions (*erga*) they perform—parts and functions first mentioned in the writings of Aristotle and his contemporaries—to be transformed into fundamental points in the doctrine of Corax, or into fundamental aspects of the human capacity for discourse which wrote themselves, as it were, into the earliest treatise on the subject.

(Highly similar lists of parts and *erga* are ascribed variously to Aristotle's friend Theodectes [Aristotle, fr. 133 Rose], "Isocrates and his followers" [B XXIV 29], Corax [B II 23], or simply to the fact that, as human beings, we are all of us "well equipped by nature for seeking the good will of those from whom a request has to be made [the task of the proem, with its *captatio benevolentiae*], setting forth what has occurred [narrative], establishing our own case and refuting that of our opponent [proof], and ending up [epilogue] with a plea for indulgence or sympathy—the whole province of oratorical skill in fact.")[22] In similar fashion, Pythagoras and Thales, as the putative founders of moral and natural philosophy, come to be credited with, respectively, the Platonic tripartition of the soul and the Aristotelian distinction between quality and substrate (11A12).

Further reason for rejecting the late antique or early Byzantine tradition about Corax will emerge later. On the other hand, the Platonic and Aristotelian reports that conflict with this tradition are themselves suspect, even if to a lesser degree and for different reasons. The vacillation they display between contempt and respect for protorhetoric is linked to a larger fluctuation, which the reconstructions offered thus far fail to take into account. Contempt is appropriate to the extent that Corax, Tisias, and their followers are seen, as they are on occasion by Plato and Aristotle, as fit subjects for ridicule; respect is linked to the feeling that they are influential enough to be dangerous. This larger fluctuation can be—and sometimes is—explained as the result of a natural tendency on the part of Plato and Aristotle to associate protorhetoric with the work of their own principal pedagogical rivals, the Sophists. The latter may not have composed formal handbooks—hence, perhaps, the distinction sometimes drawn (for example, by Plato himself at *Gorgias* 465c1–3) between rhetoric and Sophistic. On the other hand, their claim to universal expertise—to the ability to equip their pupils for dealing with any and all situations where verbal skills were required—could have been seen as leading to a similar preoccupation with the constants of the prospective speaker's technique rather than the variables of his prospective subject matter. The one was readily teachable, the other not. More important, concentration on technique made it unnecessary to face the moral issues that the success-at-any-price attitude of the Sophists raised, and which Plato and Aristotle hoped to solve by their insistence on a philosophically informed, responsible use of the techniques of persuasion. This is, conceivably, the correct explanation, even if it leaves unclear the exact character of Sophistic instruction in rhetoric. Serious concern over the amorality of the Sophists might well have coexisted, in the way suggested, with amusement at the equally amoral, but fairly harmless activities of their rhetorical contemporaries. But ridicule and warning can coexist equally well as parts of a single, two-pronged polemic; and contempt and respect can be, in similar fashion, the simultaneous contempt and respect one tries to cultivate toward a troublesome opponent. If so, the discrepancies in what Plato and Aristotle say of protorhetoric may be—in the first instance—a reflection of their authors' immediate polemical purposes, just as the position of Corax in late versions of the tradition is a reflection of doxographical obsession with first beginnings.

The polemic would have been of a very special kind, intimately bound up with the tendency, familiar enough elsewhere in Plato and Aristotle, to take into account only those elements in the achievement of one's predecessors that seem to be partial anticipations of one's own. The tradition about Corax, Tisias, and their successors goes back, at least in part, to Aristotle's own history of their teaching (the "Compendium of Arts" [*Synagōgē technōn*]); and the protorhetorical handbook, however the credit for its contents is distributed, emerges from that tradition as a work that conceives of rhetoric, by implication, in exactly the same residual, negative way as do Plato and Aristotle. It is a handbook devoted to selected aspects of the process of persuasion once its dialectical element has been removed: the formal plan of the judicial oration and the verbal and argumentative structures it contains. In writing a discussion of such turns of phrase and thought and incorporating it into a context that considers the arrangement but not the subject matter of a judicial oration, the protorhetorician is in effect clearing the way for Plato and Aristotle. He disposes of certain subsidiary problems posed by their subject—specifically rhetorical problems not requiring the expertise of a philosopher—in preparation for the ultimate assault on the major problems, which *do* require such expertise. Depending on the polemical needs of the moment, the whole enterprise may be ridiculed for its essential triviality or credited with having brought matters by gradual stages to the point where it is clear that rhetoric is much too important to be left to the rhetoricians. In just the same fashion the famous survey in *Metaphysics* A is simultaneously patronizing and contemptuous in its assessment of the pre-Socratics: they correctly perceived one of the four causes ultimately recognized by Aristotle but were unable, for the most part, to move from material cause to the investigation of formal, final, or efficient cause.

The inaccuracy of such an assessment as far as the pre-Socratics are concerned is now generally recognized,[23] as is the inaccuracy of much of the doxography attached to the names of Thales and Pythagoras. But scholars are, in general, even less inclined here than in the case of Corax to draw the obvious parallel for our conception of the history of rhetoric. They continue to view earlier writers on eloquence as, in effect, inchoate Aristotelians, ignoring the fact that, had Plato and Aristotle not chosen to introduce the idea of rhetoric in the course of polemical references to those writers, no one would ever have thought to look for its source anywhere but in their own philosophies.

The relation between a speaker's message and its verbal presentation closely parallels that between Aristotle's formal and material causes (with persuasion as a final cause guiding the agent-rhetorician's efforts to find a suitable verbal embodiment for his argument), or between Platonic form and particular instance. If the embodiment of a single idea in the acoustic structure of different languages is like the way a craftsman fashions tools out of different materials with some single model of proper functioning to guide him (Plato, *Cratylus* 389d3–90a2), the same should hold true for the way an idea is expressed in various styles or through a particular selection among the myriad ways a thing can be said to produce a given effect on a given audience.[24] As noted earlier, Aristotle's conception of poetry is essentially rhetorical, and Plato's notions about literature, insofar as they are prescriptive rather than critical, even more so. Literature's proper business is the exemplification, through hymns to gods and encomia to men (*Rep.* 10.607a3–4) of the virtues discovered and defined by philosophy; or, in the case of comedy (*Laws* 7.816d5–e10), the presentation of the ridiculous and the base in those particular manifestations that will discourage the spectator from ever wanting to imitate them himself. More generally, the relation between dialectic and rhetoric parallels that between the educational programs of *Republic* and *Laws*, or—insofar as can be determined—the mode of presentation in Aristotle's esoteric and exoteric writings. Whenever the conclusions to which philosophy leads must be made acceptable to those whose philosophical attainments are one-sided or imperfect or nonexistent,[25] or when true opinion is sought as a goal rather than the *logos* that is able to give an account of itself, or when the likeness of truth is to be presented as a substitute for truth itself, rhetoric is necessary—so necessary that, had it not existed already, Plato and Aristotle would surely have had to invent it.

To show that they did in effect invent it, and that current views of the nature of protorhetoric have been heavily influenced by their own attempt to present earlier masters of discourse and argument as minor precursors rather than serious intellectual rivals—is one purpose of this book. More generally, I seek to replace the evolutionary model of development favored by most historians with the "revolutionary" one mentioned at the beginning of this chapter, making it possible to consider the ultimately successful revolution of Plato and Aristotle, the *ancien régime* they supplanted, and what can be known or reliably inferred about their less successful revolutionary rivals in proper historical context.

For a crucial series of decades in the course of the fifth and early fourth centuries a host of Sophists, scientists, physicians, polymaths, logographers, orators, statesmen, dramatists, and exegetes disputed among themselves the position left vacant by the collapse of poetry's undisputed claims to be the moral and intellectual mentor of Greece. Victory went ultimately to the group of combatants best able to develop, first, a satisfactory (philosophical, as it turned out) alternative to the poetic world view and, second, a new form of discourse (artistic—that is, rhetorical—prose) capable of rivaling poetic performances in its power to satisfy the curiosity, engage the sympathies, and fire the imagination of an audience, whether hearers or readers. Victory also went, as matters turned out, to a group that insisted on a rigid initial separation of the two tasks, and on the strict subordination of the second to the first. The radical clarity with which Plato and Aristotle established and maintained this hierarchy sets them apart from their contemporaries and predecessors and makes them—not Tisias, Corax, and their successors—the true founders of rhetoric as well as of philosophy. Yet all were involved to one degree or another in both tasks, and all were committed, in their search for some alternative to the age-old, orally maintained dominance of poetic authority, to exploring the possibilities of the relatively new medium of written prose. These are the crucial constants of the cultural situation out of which rhetoric arose: sweeping rejection of the poets in favor of some alternative way of understanding and presenting the world, and a proliferation of written prose texts—often basically "arhetorical" in style and conception. Piecemeal progress, or inept groping, toward some of the less significant achievements later incorporated into the edifice of Platonic and Aristotelian rhetorical theory doubtless existed, but not to the extent of monopolizing the activity of any one group of writers. The possibility of presence should not distract attention from more important tasks. These are, in the next two chapters a consideration of those aspects of early Greek poetry and early attitudes toward it which impeded or anticipated the growth of rhetoric, in chapters 4–6 a reassessment of the principal "arhetorical" and protorhetorical fifth-century efforts at replacing or supplementing the hitherto dominant poetic mode, and in chapters 7–8 an examination of the ultimately decisive interaction between new intellectual movements and the new art of written prose, which was to culminate in Plato's dialogues and Aristotle's treatise—the earliest masterpieces of the Western rhetorical tradition.

It is not possible to discuss all of these topics with the thoroughness one would like, given the fact that Plato and Isocrates are the only thinkers from the critical decades whose works survive *in extenso.* Hence the scope of the present work. It is less a full-scale piece of intellectual history than an extended essay, which seeks to point out the gaps in our knowledge and the problems they pose, criticize earlier solutions, suggest new ones where possible, and, above all, indicate the dimensions of the phenomena under consideration. Like the romantic revolution that ushered it out, the set of transformations that ushered in the age of rhetoric was part of a radical, pervasive reorganization of habits and attitudes. Without some consideration of the character and course of that reorganization it is impossible to understand either the genesis of rhetoric itself or the tremendous intellectual excitement and commitment that accompanied it.

THE
PRERHETORICAL
AGE

Two

Oral Poetry and Oral Eloquence

orace was following standard rhetorical principles, tried and tested over the preceding three centuries, when he urged the aspiring dramatist to prefer a reworking of traditional themes to striking out on his own:

> Better Homer restaged for yet another time
> Than matters unassayed in prose or rhyme.
> (*Ars Poetica* 129–30)

Greeks of the archaic and classical periods felt—or at least expressed themselves—rather differently. It is always the latest tale that wins a singer applause, says Telemachus (*Odyssey* 1.351–52); and his father—the greatest of Homeric tale-tellers—is of the same opinion. "Once properly told, a tale should not be repeated," is Odysseus's final remark to Alcinous (12.452–53), following the long narrative of adventure that fills four books of the poem. Three centuries later Pindar still sings the virtues of "old wine and new song" (*Olympian* 9.48), and his younger contemporary Bacchylides (fr. 5) complains of the difficulty of having to find one's way to the gates of songs unsung by others. Later still, the complaint is echoed by the epic poet Choerilos of Samos, a contemporary of

Socrates (fr. 1 p. 250 Powell). Isocrates was to disagree, strongly and often, but he belongs to a later generation.

The Muse who presides over the poet's craft is not a personification of his powers of verbal elaboration and variation. She is one of the daughters of Mnemosyne ("Memory" or—more accurately, perhaps, since the memory involved is not simply that of individual poet or listener—"Information Retrieval"). Her patronage sets the poet apart as one who has access, whether through bardic tradition or some other, supernatural means, to knowledge of things ordinary mortals do not know, and of which they learn for the first time through him. She is accordingly asked to reveal the identity and size of all the Greek contingents that made up Agamemnon's host at Troy (*Iliad* 2.484–93); it is her instruction of the Phaeacian poet Demodocus that enables him to tell the story of what happened at Troy as if he had been present or spoken to an eyewitness (*Odyssey* 8.488–92); she and her sisters can sing to the poet not only of what is and was but what is to come (Hesiod, *Theogony* 32); and her fellow singers the Sirens have a similar claim on men's attention: they know "all the toils the gods brought upon Argives and Trojans at broad-plained Troy," and "all things that come to pass over the face of rich-bearing earth" (*Odyssey* 12.189–91).

The information supplied from these sources is often of moral as well as practical value; it is not required to be either, however. The poet's recitation may simply satisfy curiosity or distract the mind from troubles. But once conveyed, its message has no need of being repeated—unless, of course, the hearer forgets, in which case it is Information Retrieval in the form of Reminder rather than Memory that is working through the agency of the Muse.

There is also no need—until the late fifth century—to find fault with poets for the form in which their message is couched. Critics charge that what poets say is untrue, or impossible, or improbable, or inconsistent, or trivial, or morally harmful, or concerned with matters about which someone other than the poet could speak with greater authority. No poet is criticized for being dull, or prosaic, or clumsy, or unclear, or for botching a theme handled well by someone else. Even Plato himself, in the works that antedate the *Phaedrus*, seems singularly uninterested in any arguments that would give a poet credit for more successful or effective presentation of material available in different form elsewhere. The rhapsode Ion readily grants Socrates' contention that the purpose of poetry is the transmission of information on chariot driving, military tactics, navigation, and the like (*Ion* 537a1 ff.); but upon being asked why poet or rhapsode rather than charioteer or general or pilot should be the one in charge of such transmissions, he is not allowed to make the (to us) obvious answer that the rhapsode's presentation is often more attractive, more readily absorbed, and more easily remembered. And the entire condemnation of poetry (*Republic* 10) as an imitation of an imitation rests on the assumption that if one is familiar with an original the varying methods and varying degrees of success with which it is imitated cannot be of any possible interest or value to an observer.

What is said explicitly in praise or disparagement of poetry is in line with what is implied by the similes and metaphors used in connection with it. The comparison of a well-conceived, well-composed work of art to a well-proportioned living body appears in Plato's *Phaedrus* (264c2–5) and is ubiquitous thereafter—for very understandable reasons. It suggests a basic skeleton or musculature of content fleshed out in rhetorical fashion with illustrations and elaborations and finally given a suitable epidermis of words. But there is no trace of the comparison earlier than the *Phaedrus*. The equally rhetorical idea of presenting ideas in appropriate "dress" does happen to be attested earlier, but in the form of an explicit comparison. Aristophanes (*Frogs* 1057–60) defends Aeschylean grandiosity by saying that a poet's language (*rhēmata*) should match the sentiments and thoughts (*gnōmai* and *dianoiai*) of his characters, just as "clothes worn by demigods are larger than those of ordinary men." The notion was evidently new enough to the poet's audience that it needed some sort of gloss to make it clear. Gorgias's definition (*Helen* 9) of poetry as "nothing other than words with the addition of meter" shows a similar need to stress the (to us) obvious idea that verse is prose in metrical dress.

A similar idea appears in Plato when he likens the poet (*Politicus* 277b6) to a painter overlaying a line drawing with shading or color; and the *pictura/poesis* analogy may well be earlier than either

Gorgias or Aristophanes. Tradition, at any rate, ascribes it to Simonides (*apud* Plut. *De glor. Ath.* 3.346 ff.; cf. fr. 190b Bergk). But there is no reason to believe that Simonides would have used the comparison in the way Plato does—to make the poet a mere decorator of surfaces. The latter idea is, moreover, clearly excluded when the artistic constructions to which a poem is likened are the solidly homogeneous ones of sculpture (Pindar, *Nemean* 1.1, *Isthmian* 2.45–56) and architecture (Pindar, *Pythian* 3.114, 6.78, fr. 194). What Pindar compares to a far-shining architectural facade (*Olympian* 6.1–4) is simply the first thing in a poem that confronts a hearer—its opening words or stanza—not a resplendent overlay of poetic decoration. Similarly, it is the whole content of Nestor's speech that Homer likens to honey or something sweeter. There is no trace of Aristotle's idea of stylistic or melodic sweetening (*hēdysma*) added to the substance of a piece of poetry or prose (*Rhet.* 3.3 1406a19, *Poetics* 6.1450b16–17).

The attitude that lies behind the statements and comparisons cited is perfectly compatible with the well-documented tendency of archaic poets to write in a highly traditional manner, producing their "new" songs by recombining or repeating with minor variations stereotyped verbal formulas, scenes, and episodes. What is involved in compositions of this sort is more a traditional idiom than a traditional style, and its presence no more commits poets to a rhetorical view of composition than unconscious adherence to a fixed vocabulary, syntax, and set of conversational clichés commits everyday spoken discourse to such a view. The underlying poetic grammar is transformational rather than paradigmatic: a set of procedures for generating new poetic utterances through successive substitutions in a given combination of words, events, or episodes while avoiding poetic solecism. Movement is from one particular to another, not to a fresh realization, with a new set of particulars, of some independently existing pattern whose basic character remains unchanged throughout. To think of it in the latter fashion distorts the psychology of the whole process—as does Aristotle's recipe (see chapter 1) for composing a tragedy.

Even when there is an effort to draw an explicit contrast between what is essential and constant in a poet's work and what is arbitrary and variable, the distinction does not seem to be drawn along rhetorical lines. Pindar speaks on occasion (*Nemean* 4.33; *Olympian* 7.89 and 13.29) of the "terms" or "ordinance" (*tethmos*) under which he is composing an epinician ode, evidently referring to information about people, places, and victories whose inclusion was stipulated by the commissioner of the poem as part of his original contract with the author. And the Sophist Gorgias concludes his so-called defense of Helen by using an almost synonymous term ("law" [*nomos*]) to refer to the basic task he has set himself in the speech. What seems to be involved in both instances is not so much the subject of a composition as the rules of a game, an external constraint on the poet's activity that specifies the *sine qua non* for successful completion of his commission. Once the *sine qua non* is present the rest of the work is not elaboration of a theme but free exercise of his craft as strikes the poet's fancy.

Not surprisingly, poems and genres are regularly identified by reference to one or more of these external constraints: circumstances of performance (a maidens' song, or "partheneion," a processional hymn or "prosodion," etc.), meter ("the trimeters of Archilochus"), protagonist (the "Odysseus poem"), or setting (the "Ilium poem")—much more rarely by reference to what we would think of as a theme (*The Sack of Troy, The Heroes' Returns*). For us, as well as for the poet himself in one passage (*Nemean* 4.78), the Pindaric ode is a song "on the subject of victory" (*epinikios*); but Pindar's preferred way of referring to it is as a "carouse" (*kōmos*) or song "to accompany a carouse" (*epikōmios*).

Even the most common later word for the plot of a play (*hypothesis*) may have had originally the same circumscribing rather than defining force that attaches to *tethmos* and *nomos*. In its earliest attestations it refers to a geometrical or dialectical hypothesis: a "foundation laying" (*hypotithenai*) of those basic assumptions whose tentative acceptance is a ground for the elaboration, examination, or testing that is to follow. In the case of a drama, the hypothesis would be the assumptions that the audience must make if what they see and hear on stage is to make sense: first, that the actors are a given set of characters from history or mythology; and second, that what they do and say on stage are the acts and words of that set of characters at some particular time and place in the past. The dramatist may compose whatever he likes, so long as it follows, in some way or other, from this basic hypothesis. Even in those situations where the hypothesis included the outlines of legends with which an audience was familiar it would, like *nomos* and *tethmos,* function as a means of providing limits, rather than an actual guide, to the exercise of the poet's talent. Different "treatments" of the Orestes or Oedipus myths might thus be better described as different playings of the Oedipus or Orestes game with—as often in games—prizes for the person whose play is best.[1]

No writer earlier than Plato suggests that the distribution of these prizes should be determined by how well or how badly different playings of the game approximate or embody some canonical version, whether in historical tradition or earlier play or dramatic theory. The dramatist is a creator or "maker" (*poiētēs*) of words, not—as he is for Aristotle—an imitator of things; and theater is a doing or action (*drama*), not a representation.[2] If epic narrative under the patronage of the Muse makes the poet into an eyewitness of what he cannot in fact have seen or heard, drama works the same transformation, but on the audience rather than the author. The unsophisticated doubtless attributed this to some sort of magic; others—by natural extension of the contract metaphor—might have regarded it as the fulfillment of an unstated agreement between dramatist and public. The dramatist was thereby pledged to do his best to deceive the audience into thinking—for the duration of the performance—that they were seeing and hearing what they could never have seen or heard; and the audience was similarly pledged not to resist this effort at deception. This is evidently the line of reasoning behind Gorgias's famous assertion (B 23) that tragedy is a "just deception" and one in which "those who are deceived are wiser than those who are not."[3]

The earliest Greek eloquence, no less than the earliest Greek poetry, depends heavily for its success on the degree to which it creates the impression of eyewitness immediacy or accuracy. This is the source—so far as the samples provided allow one to judge—of the most eloquent Homeric hero's ability to "speak lies like truth" (*Odyssey* 19.203). When Odysseus tells one of these lies his technique is to accumulate such a wealth of circumstantial detail that the whole thing seems too complicated to have been invented. The method has something in common with the later device known as *evidentia* (Lausberg 810): re-creation of a scene with such vividness as to compel belief on the part of the hearer. But *evidentia* is a characteristic piece of rhetorical indirectness: an artful means of insisting on the truth of a particular version of what happened while seeming merely to describe it. Odysseus's narratives lack the conscious focus of their rhetorical counterparts and quickly become indistinguishable from any good storyteller's exercise of his gift for creating a wealth of exciting incidents or interesting characters of some complexity. The unfolding of an entire story always eclipses in importance the particular falsehood for the purpose of which it was invented. The audience is never encouraged, as it is by the orator or the Aristotelian playwright when he seeks to confer plausibility on a *mythos* or a *narratio*, to focus on a central point and disregard the rest of the narrative except insofar as it reinforces that point. And when such focusing does occur, Odysseus's lies may cease to be persuasive. Penelope is convinced of the truth of the disguised Odysseus's account of his meeting with her husband because of specific signs requested by her (19.215–19) and supplied by Odysseus. The vividness of the whole narrative (19.165–202) is not enough to persuade her. And Eumaeus accepts everything in Odysseus's fictitious account of his own adventures (14.192–359) except one of the key points of the whole narrative; namely, that there is good reason to believe Odysseus is still alive (14.363–65). Since the speech to Eumaeus fails to persuade and the speech to Penelope needs supplementary confirmation before it can do so, both would have to be considered failures as rhetoric. Yet obviously they do not affect—and probably are intended to confirm—Odysseus's position as master of the lie like truth.

Odyssean eloquence is equally unsuccessful, by rhetorical standards, in transmitting the content of Agamemnon's offers of amends to Achilles. The offer is reported verbatim, with one exception: the concluding insistence (*Iliad* 9.158–61) that, in return for the extensive material compensation he is to receive, Achilles recognize Agamemnon's preeminence in the Greek host. A true rhetorician would surely have attempted a bit of tactful rephrasing at this point. Odysseus handles the situation by simply leaving out the offensive codicil. Iris exercises the same sort of censorship when she refuses to convey Poseidon's angry suggestion (*Iliad* 15.185–99) that Zeus cease ordering his brothers around as if they were inferiors and confine himself to the province that the three-way division of sky, sea, and underworld among the sons of Cronus assigned to him. Censorship here leads to a total abandonment of the original message and the replacement of defiance by acquiescence: Poseidon agrees, under protest, to abide by Zeus's decision to help the Trojans (*Iliad* 15.212–17). Neither this passage nor the parallel one in *Iliad* 9 describes reformulation of a message in such a way as to secure its better acceptance. If there is rhetoric present at all, it is the art, not of speaking, but of leaving things unspoken—and unimplied.

What does come out in Homeric speech is eloquence: a combination of volubility, native gift for holding the attention of an audience, and a mind well stocked with accurate memories and sound counsels (the prerhetorical orator's counterpart to the vision of past, present, and future which the Muses give the poet). Reservations about the value of this combination are expressed quite early, but in a context in which possession of "a tongue that speaks sweetly" (Tyrtaeus 12.8) is simply another instance—along with strength, size, fleetness of foot, wealth, beauty, power—of a natural quality or external possession that is not worth having unless accompanied by bravery in battle.

The picture of "prerhetorical" Greece offered thus far runs a certain risk of being oversimplified or one-sided, and it is certainly incomplete insofar as one circumscribed, but important, area of discourse is concerned (see chapter 3). The role, or nonrole, it envisions for rhetoric can be strikingly paralleled, however, in a tradition of poetic composition that has been studied repeatedly over the last half-century because of the light it sheds on the character of early Greek epic. The oral poets of modern Yugoslavia have no easy way of referring to, or thinking about, different versions of a single theme or story. Depending on the situation, two different versions are likely to be described, now as totally different, now as identical "word for word."[4] The phenomenon is mostly simply explained as a result of the character of the poets' medium: improvised oral performance. Without the possibility of fixing the details of a given version in writing so that they can be compared with those of another one, it is difficult to establish the existence of any middle ground between identity and total dissimilarity, and even more difficult to isolate the set of shared motifs which allows two divergent performances to be linked together as separate versions of the same piece of narrative subject matter.

The basically "arhetorical" character of early Greek views of artistic discourse is explicable, in part, in the same way. Greek poetry was, in origin, a completely oral form of communication, and the attitudes fostered by orality persisted well beyond the period (first quarter of the seventh century B.C.) during which writing first began to be used for recording certain types of poetic texts. We cannot be sure, of course, that a Greek oral poet would have dealt with the idea of different poetic presentations of a single theme in the same way as his modern Yugoslav counterparts. But something about his attitude can be inferred from the fact that the related notion of the work of a single poet given different renditions over the years by different bards is foreign to the Greek mentality in its earliest stages. The earliest such rendition of which we have any record involves a written text of the Homeric *Hymn to Delian Apollo* delivered by the rhapsode Cynaithos in 512 B.C. (Scholia to Pindar, *Isthmian* 2.1c p. 29.13 Drachmann).[5] Until the term *poiētēs* (first attested in the mid-fifth century) gained currency, the language did not even have the means of distinguishing composer from performer. All poets are simply "singers" (*aoidoi*) and every singer draws directly on the Muse, not on one of his own predecessors, for the content of his performance.

What performers of later ages receive from those predecessors usually includes, as it did for Cynaithos, one or more written poetic texts; and this link with writing—or the absence thereof—may help explain a further "antirhetorical" element in early Greek attitudes toward discourse. The rhetorical mentality, which recognizes the possibility and necessity of communicating a single message in different ways, is also a mentality that sees the process of communication as in some sense problematic. Whether because of the limited abilities of most speakers, or the inherent uncertainty of things to be communicated, or the ignorance and obstinacy of most audiences, one cannot assume that the recipient of a message will necessarily respond to the same things and in the same way as the speaker intends. This is a basic consideration underlying and explaining the deviousness, indirectness, and hyperadequacy of rhetorical expression: the detours, overshootings, recapitulations, and repetitions that have been the subject of rhetorical analysis for more than two thousand years. Before such a view of communication came into being—and its earliest clear manifestations in Greece do not antedate the sixth century—rhetorical uses of language, though doubtless as old, individually, as Greek itself, were unlikely ever to appear in sufficient concentration to produce a characteristic mode of discourse or allow it to be thought of as such.[6]

There is no gulf between the world of thought and that of reality in the Homeric age. To know is simply to perceive (*noein*).[7] And there is even less of a gap between a thought and its verbalization or reception. A speech is an uttered thought, a thought a speech that remains for some reason or other unuttered. Speaking and thinking have the same contrary: acting; and so far from being set in opposition to each other they are often subsumed under a single word (the verb *phrazein*, for example, which means either "think," "devise" or "tell," "communicate"). The word to "say" and the word to "mean" are the same (*legein*), different verbs only appearing later or in reference to situations where, for one reason or another, what is said is totally incomprehensible: utterances in a foreign language, written messages in a script one cannot read (*Iliad* 6.168), oracles (Heraclitus B93). Once reported as direct discourse, a speech is rarely if ever repeated in the form of a paraphrase or summary. Restatement and rephrasing of this sort only becomes normal as part of the search for meaning that is conducted in the Socratic dialogue. The typically Homeric utterance (*epos*) is "winged" in that it is posted full speed to its destination and so taken in and understood without any difficulty. It is possible to be guilty of utterance that misfires or is off target (*[aph]amartoepes* [*Iliad* 3.215, 13.824]), but in that case the target missed is the truth, not the understanding of an interlocutor. It is only later (Pindar *Pythian* 6.37, *Olympian* 9.12) that we hear of words that are "ground-sped" (*chamaipetes*); and their occurrence is a rare and random one. The fact that for one reason or another an utterance fails to be taken in and so falls to the ground is no reflection on the character of the words themselves or that of their speaker. It simply happens that people occasionally forget or neglect or fail to understand what is said; there is no way to frame a communication in such a way as to minimize or eliminate the possibility of such occurrences.

Speakers are contrasted in the epic by reference to how much they say, rather than to degree of rhetorical competence. Menelaus (*Iliad* 3.212–15) and Ajax are said, or show themselves, to be men of few words, but there is no suggestion that their words are ever inadequate to the situation. And similarly, though Odysseus is a man of many words, this merely means that when he speaks he is concerned with topics that require lengthy exposition—such as the details of Agamemnon's conciliatory offer in Book 9 of the *Iliad*. His speech on that occasion (9.225–306) contrasts strikingly with Ajax's brief reproach to Achilles for his indifference to the lives of his comrades (9.624–42), but what the contrast brings out is the difference between the two men and the two sets of considerations, not that between heartfelt brevity and diplomatic long-windedness in the presentation of the same request. Ajax is not "tongue-tied" (*aglōssos*), as he is in Pindar's later account (*Nemean* 8.24) of the contest for the arms of Achilles, nor is Odysseus a master of the "flashy lie" (*aiolōi pseudei* [*Nemean* 8.25]). In *Iliad* 9 Odyssean diplomacy involves only omission, not expansion. Nestor's speeches can be faulted—if they are intended to be faulted at all—for being, at most, longer than the occasions on which they are delivered demand; they are not regarded as inflations of dull or small matters into something large or momentous. Direct transmissions of intentional falsehood—the straightforward and hence unrhetorical lie (see chapter 1)—is never contrasted with what is rhetorically exaggerated, devious, misleading; both are simply instances of untruths (*pseudē*).

The prevalence of a nonproblematic view of communication— like the early Greek preoccupation with the purely informative aspects of discourse discussed before—is probably a phenomenon closely linked to the absence of written texts. We are dealing here with interrelated aspects of an "arhetorical" culture. In this instance, however, the link with orality may be accounted for in different ways, depending on the relative weight one assigns to two contrasting aspects of written communication: its fixity on the one hand and, on the other, its ambiguity. Writing entrusts communication to a set of verbal signifiers that remain (or with proper care can remain) constant through an unlimited number of transmissions. The freedom of this medium from the distortion that accompanies transmission by word of mouth inevitably calls attention to the possibility or likelihood of such distortion, and so increases receptivity to any art which, like rhetoric, teaches how to guard against—or utilize—such possibilities.

This is the phenomenon that is the starting point for one of the two most valuable inquiries into the contrasting effects of oral and written media on verbal discourse that have been conducted in this century. The inquiry was inaugurated in 1963 by E. A. Havelock's *Preface to Plato*.[8] The other line of inquiry, begun in the same decade by Jacques Derrida's *De la grammatologie* (1967) takes what seems at first glance an exactly opposite view of those effects.[9] If a written message is much less subject to distortion when a series of transmissions is involved, any single transmission by means of writing involves certain ambiguities from which oral communications are largely free. It usually occurs apart from any situational context, without the clarification that intonation, phrasing, gesture, and other aspects of delivery bring, and without the presence of the transmitter to explain, rephrase, and repeat in an effort to minimize or correct misunderstanding. And the very visibility and tangibleness of the written document reifies the medium through which communication takes place, thereby producing a heightened awareness of its existence and the possibility for distortion that this brings.

The coexistence of oral and written media of communication doubtless had the further effect of calling attention to the peculiar shortcomings of each, and the founders of the fourth-century Athenian philosophical schools took both sets of considerations into account. They entrusted their doctrines to, on the one hand, an extensive body of written texts and, on the other, to a vigorous tradition of oral discussion and dialectic between scholarch and pupils which was passed on from one generation to the next and made advanced philosophical study impossible anywhere but at Athens. Rhetoric itself, as it finally crystallized in the fourth century, also draws in different but significant ways on the resources of both spoken and written word. And the same applies to the dissemination of literature and ideas throughout the Hellenistic age.

It was only in the early centuries of the Christian era that the balance finally shifted definitively in favor of the written word—in response to its obvious superiority as a means of communication within the ecumenical world of pagan or Christian Rome, to the advent of new religions deriving their authority from a finite body of fixed written texts, and also, one suspects, to the replacement of the papyrus roll by the far more efficient and convenient means of written communication provided by the codex.

As in ancient times, both the Havelockian and Derridesque perspectives on the relationship between oral and written communication need to be taken into consideration—often, as in the present instance, simultaneously. Both lines of argument help to establish the probability of a causal connection between the predominantly oral character of early Greek culture and its arhetorical conception of discourse as a transparent medium through which language performs its largely informative function easily and efficiently.[10]

That conception becomes, of course, less universal and less pronounced as one passes on to later phases of the "prerhetorical" era. The middle of the fifth century has already appeared several times as a *terminus ante quem* for the generalizations of this chapter.

Earlier attitudes were modified under the influence of the Sophistic enlightenment and in response to the vastly increased role that political and juridical eloquence played in Syracuse and Athens, the two most populous cities of the Greek world in the second half of the century. These modifications, though slower to take effect and less far-reaching at first than the standard accounts of the history of rhetoric claim, will receive detailed treatment, beginning in chapter 4. It would be misleading, however, to end the discussion of the prerhetorical age without some attention to another area of discourse, in which—atypically—a rhetoric of sorts had been in vogue among the Greeks from the beginning. The differences between this incipient or partial rhetoric and the fully developed, all-pervasive discipline of the fourth century are as instructive as the similarities.

Three

Tact and Etiquette

The Chinese *Book of Etiquette and Ceremonial*, traditionally ascribed to Confucius, prescribes that, upon successful conclusion of a betrothal, the following exchange should take place between the contracting parties:

Father of Bride-to-be: Since your honor has come on business to my house, I use the custom of ancient time, and ask to be allowed, as an assistant, to offer you a glass of wine.

Messenger (acting for Father of Groom-to-be): Since the business which I have come upon is already finished, I venture to decline the honor.

Father: According to the custom of the ancients, I venture to press my invitation.

Messenger: Since I cannot secure permission to decline, dare I do other than obey?[1]

Anyone familiar with the basic forms taken by communication in the West will have no difficulty in identifying this dialogue as a piece of "fossilized" rhetoric. The host's message ("Have a glass of wine before you leave") and the guest's reply ("I will") are both transmitted in such a way as to prevent any interference that might arise from the offer's seeming peremptory and self-important, or the acceptance presumptuous and overly eager. The rhetoric is frozen or "fossilized" in that it excludes variation in response to elements in one betrothal situation not present in another; but it is probably more effective for that very reason. Fossilization gives to the whole exchange the sound, and authority, of tradition. It is something more than just a skillful avoidance of misunderstandings about the spirit in which an offer is being made and accepted.

One may call discourse of this sort the rhetoric of tact and etiquette. It is encountered fairly frequently in non-Western societies—more frequently than in the West, perhaps, and with a higher level of sophistication. Formulas of politeness are more important, more elaborate, more susceptible to variation stemming from the roles of speaker and addressee; and literary discourse is distinguished from nonliterary discourse by a much more thoroughly worked out set of conventions. The latter, like the formulas of etiquette, owe at least part of their success to the simple fact that they are a kind of code, and that an ability to manipulate and understand the code sets transmitter and recipient apart as members of a special elite.

To judge from the survey accounts now available, non-Western discourse contains very little outside this fairly restricted area that can be classified as rhetoric.[2] And the situation in the arhetorical societies of Asia and Africa is strikingly parallel to that in the prerhetorical society of early Greece. For there, too, a rhetoric of etiquette and tact exists, one which is fairly rudimentary by oriental standards but which resembles its oriental counterpart in that it is a virtually isolated phenomenon within its cultural context.

Greek instances tend to be veiled and allusive, not simply circuitous and indirect like the Chinese example cited. They also tend to appear in situations that call for originality as well as knowledge of frozen formulas. The speaker is usually an inferior seeking to answer or advise or petition a superior without seeming arrogant, or to praise him without seeming obsequious. "Slaves," says Aristotle (*Rhet.* 3.14 1415b23–24), "are in the habit of talking around rather than to the question, and not coming to the point right away." (His example is the guard's speech to Creon in the *Antigone*). The simplest form of such "slave" discourse was, according to tradition, the invention of the slave Aesop; and it was employed with enough characteristically rhetorical self-consciousness that it received a name of its own: *ainos*. It was also, at least initially, a characteristically rhetorical discourse *ad hominem:* the earliest instances of the genre all have a particular individual as their addressee.[3]

Not every *ainos,* of course, is a beast fable told by a slave. The word can be applied to any story that means more or other than what it says (the Greek word for riddle—*aenigma*—comes from the same root).[4] Poets and heroes may resort to *ainos* when a sufficient difference exists between their status and that of the person being addressed. The earliest attested occurrence involves the disguised Odysseus, who is unwilling to criticize the hospitality of his host Eumaeus, to whom he stands somewhat in the relationship of a suppliant, by asking directly for a cloak to sleep under for the night. He makes his request through the story of how, one night on patrol, his commander "Odysseus" saved him from freezing to death by getting a younger member of the party to volunteer to run an errand—expecting, as in fact occurred, that the man would leave his cloak behind and someone else would be able to use it. Eumaeus congratulates Odysseus on the excellence of his *ainos* (14.508) and assures him that he will not lack warm covering for the night.

The next attested appearance of the word is in connection with Hesiod's story of the hawk and the nightingale in *Works and Days* 202 ff. Though the import of the story is obscure, it obviously means more than it says; and it is directed at a superior—an *ainos,* Hesiod calls it, for princes who understand.

The poet most frequently put in the position of having to address princes and kings was, of course, Pindar; and more examples of the rhetoric of tact come from him than from any other archaic author. The animal paradigm associated with the fable—though not the term *ainos* itself—occurs in a brief, highly obscure piece of advice to King Hieron of Syracuse at the end of the second *Pythian* (72–97). Hieron is also the addressee, in the third *Pythian,* of the single most elaborate piece of rhetoric that has survived from the archaic age. In this poem the king, already ill with a disease that was eventually to prove fatal, is given a combination of exhortation and consolation. The basic message is fairly blunt: do not, Hieron, seek to avoid the misfortune that is the common lot of humankind; to do so comes dangerously near the sin of longing for the impossible. You should think instead of how much more than the normal share of good fortune you have. The impact of this admonition is softened, however, by the way the message is introduced. It follows a long preface whose two myths illustrate in different ways the dangers of longing for the impossible. Apollo's mistress Coronis was killed by the god when, foolishly thinking her infidelity could go undiscovered, she took another lover; and her son Asclepius was similarly slain by Zeus for attempting to bring a dead man back to life. The indirectness of the method is increased by the way the ode manages to suggest, until the last possible minute, that the person at whom the implicit moral of these stories is directed is not Hieron but the poet, either speaking in his own person or as a representative of the citizenry in general, and longing—like everyone else—for the miracle that would restore the king to health.[5]

The second major Pindaric exercise in tact is the longest poem in the extant collection of his works (*Pythian* 4). Its message is a plea for the reinstatement of an exile at the court of Arkesilas, king of Cyrene, prefaced by a long myth glorifying the ancestors of the king, one of whom went with Jason and the Argonauts in quest of the Golden Fleece. In the telling of this episode Jason is credited with precisely those qualities that the king himself will be asked to display: generosity to erstwhile enemies and healing restraint in putting an end to civil discord. Arkesilas is thereby prepared for the message well before it comes. The extreme length of the poem, combined with the fact that—like most epinicians—it was performed at a victory banquet may point to the existence of persuasion on other levels as well. We know little about drinking customs on such occasions; but on the reasonable assumption that the wine bowl made the rounds of the table repeatedly, returning to where it started at the end of each of the identical musical and rhythmical movements that compose the poem, Arkesilas was taking his thirteenth turn at it by the time the poem finally concludes—and so in a mood to grant almost any request a poet might care to make. The persuasion would have been no less effective for employing what rhetoricians at a later date came to call "nonartful" methods (*atechnoi pisteis*)—methods whose availability results from the accidents of the situation rather than the speaker's own verbal skill. And the persuasion would have been no less appropriate for being, as some scholars assume, imitation rather than real—part of an elaborate public charade in which Arkesilas was prevailed upon to do what he had already made up his mind to do beforehand.

The interpretation of a third rhetorical poem, Pindar's seventh *Nemean,* is rather more complicated. Ancient commentators say that it contains an apology to an Aiginetan audience for uncomplimentary references to the Aiginetan hero Neoptolemus which Pindar was alleged to have made in an earlier poem, the sixth *Paean,* composed for performance at Delphi. If the commentators are right the poem is another instance of archaic tact. It offers, moreover, the earliest extended example in Greek of the same story retold with the rhetorical demands of a new situation in mind. *Paean* 6.105–20 had been so constructed that its Delphic audience would see the avenging hand of Apollo in every stage of the voyage from Troy to Delphi that ended in Neoptolemus's death. *Nemean 7.* 33–47 presents exactly the same series of stages in completely different fashion—as a natural prelude to the solemn burial of Neoptolemus in Apollo's precinct and the heroic honors subsequently paid to him there. Elsewhere in the poem, however, the poet's tact is exercised with such subtle regard for the sensitivities of all concerned that it is now almost impossible to unravel the way it was supposed to work.[6]

Passing on from specific poems, one finds what may be evidence of a different kind of tact operating behind many of the conventions of the entire epinician genre. It was evidently expected that an athletic victor share the focus of attention with a whole range of competitors (gods and the blessings for which they are entreated, mythical heroes and their exploits, relatives victorious on other occasions). And praise had to be mingled with general observations on achievement, or sobering reflections on the folly of reaching too high and the danger that attends the great. In adhering to such conventions Pindar may be deliberately keeping the victor out of the center of attention—understating his praises or conferring them indirectly through praise of others (relatives, local heroes, tutelary gods) linked to him. He thereby avoids offending the envious or disappointed in the audience, or making the victor seem so superhumanly gifted or fortunate that even a spectator with no personal reasons for resentment might begin to feel annoyed—rather like the unknown Athenian who voted for the ostracism of Aristides simply through weariness with hearing him called "the Just." The very elaborateness of such conventions allows the poet to strengthen his appeal, in a way characteristic of the rhetoric of etiquette, to the vanity of his audience. Pindar's hearers are members of a select company of discerning men (*sophoi*) and as such ideally and uniquely qualified to read his messages right.[7]

This interpretation is in harmony with what has been, since the early 1960s, the most influential school of Pindaric criticism.[8] Yet it runs the risk of exaggerating the degree to which Pindar was concerned simply with conveying praise of an individual in the form most acceptable to a specific audience.[9] Many of his general observations may be better taken at face value: as efforts to put what an individual has done into the context of a general appreciation of agonistic achievement, its past and future as well as its present, and its costs and disappointments as well as its splendors. But however vital rhetoric may have been to the whole program, the program itself is a peculiarly Pindaric one. Elsewhere, even in Bacchylides, the only other author whose epinicians survive, archaic poetry favors the directness, clarity, openness, and frankness of aristocratic equals conversing with one another over the courtier's guarded intimations and innuendos—the "figured speech" of later theory.[10] And even in Pindar, rhetoric rarely moves beyond the area of etiquette and tact. Though devoted to praise, the genre in his hands shows little trace of the standard procedures of amplification catalogued and discussed in connection with the encomiastic oratory of later times, where dwelling on the excellence of ancestors, or native city, or the desirability of excellence itself, are fairly obvious means of indirectly exalting the central object of one's praise—or, alternatively, focusing attention elsewhere, so that shortcomings will be neglected or ignored.

Pindar, by contrast, composes for public occasions at which the simple fact of victory has, for the moment, done more than anything the poet can say to exalt the subject of his song. His discourse presupposes as its point of departure a situation in which flawless merit is receiving its full measure of recognition—just as the formulas of etiquette presuppose perfect breeding on the part of all parties involved. The poet's task is to see to it that nothing is allowed to call these initial assumptions into question—hence his often expressed preoccupation with the proper moment (*kairos*) for talking and ceasing to talk about a given aspect of his subject matter. This fear of saying too little or too much and at the wrong time was to become one of rhetoric's concerns—but only one concern among many—when it dealt with the subject of stylistic appropriateness (*prepon, decorum*). And the poet's positive contribution, by contrast with that of the orator, is a composition that in and of itself enhances the entertainment value of the occasion—not a piece of rhetoric that leaves the audience with a higher opinion of the merits of the victor than it would have had otherwise. When Pindar and Bacchylides are composing to celebrate the same athlete's victory (as they do in three surviving pairs of poems: *Olympian* 1 and Bacchylides 5; *Pythian* 1 and Bacchylides 4; *Nemean* 5 and Bacchylides 13) there is little except the presence in both poems of the name of victor and contest that indicates the fact. It is impossible to detect in any of the three pairs a particular set of shared themes that each poet is consciously developing in his own way.

That Pindaric—or epinician—rhetoric, limited range notwithstanding, was nevertheless a significant ancestor of fourth-century developments is just conceivable in itself. Similarities are undeniable between Pindar's role as tactful observer and purveyor of advice and requests to tyrant kings in the first half of the fifth century and the orator's role as advice-giver to tyrant demos in the first half of the fourth. One ancient account (A V 16) even links Corax explicitly to the Sicilian tyrants. He was an associate (*paradynasteuōn*) of theirs who somehow managed to survive the revolution that resulted in the exiling of his erstwhile colleagues and to adapt himself to the new environment of democratic Syracuse. Seeing that what had availed to manipulate a single tyrant would not work for the whole demos, he set about inventing an art—rhetoric—which would allow him to control (*rythmizesthai*) the new master as easily as the old.

Yet this development, though conceivable, does not seem to have been the one that actually took place. The epinician genre in which the rhetoric of tact is most elaborately displayed either degenerates into triviality or disappears altogether in the generation following Pindar's. Its procedures were, as it turned out, less easy to transfer to assembly and lawcourts than the ancient account just mentioned would suggest. Perhaps the populace was too insensitive, both to the finer nuances of insult that the courtier poet had to avoid and to the finer forms of suggestion and indirection that he took to avoid them. Or the lines of battle in public debate may have been more sharply drawn and the resulting decisions more fraught with consequences. In either case, the guidance required would have to have been more forthright, and the persuasive means of the speaker more compelling, both intellectually and emotionally.

Whatever the reasons, the debt owed by later rhetoric to the conventions of etiquette found in late archaic poetry is minimal—largely confined to minor formal features in epideictic oratory and a tendency to consider certain types of occasion more suitable for verbal embellishment than others.[11] For the true ancestors of the all-encompassing theory of discourse that rhetoric was ultimately to supply one must look elsewhere: from poets to the critics of the poetic tradition, and to the various defenses of poetry that their criticism brought into being.

Four

Allegory and Rhetoric

A critical attitude toward the traditional view of the nature of the world and human history handed down by the poets is first attested in Xenophanes of Colophon (second half of the sixth century), and its influence was to become in the course of the next two hundred years all but universal among educated Greeks. But poets, chroniclers, and their audiences responded in different ways to the critics' insistence that large portions of the tradition be rejected as untrue, grotesque, exaggerated, and by implication, immoral. Some of them simply complied, with or without an attempt to explain why the offensive material had come to be accepted in the first place or to remain accepted for so long. Though associated with the rationalism of Ionian historiography, cosmology, and natural philosophy, this attitude is by no means confined to that tradition. Pindar is working with standard rationalizing techniques when he dismisses the cannibal feast at which Pelops was partially eaten by the gods as a tale going back to slanderous gossip spread by neighbors when they were unable to explain the boy's sudden disappearance from his father's house (*Olympian* 1.46–51). It is only Pindar's account (1.36–45) of what actually happened (young Pelops spirited off to Olympus to be the

55

lover of the infatuated god Poseidon) that would have seemed to an Ionian every bit as absurd as the original story was outrageous. The earliest attested example of such rationalization, Stesichorus's (or Hesiod's) rejection of the tradition that made Helen an adulteress, involves a similar combination of the plausible (Helen's abduction to remote, seldom-visited Egypt) and the fantastic (Helen's ghostly look-alike that accompanied Paris to Troy).

The rationalizing approach involves a radical rewriting of mythological and historical traditions. The alternative was to keep the tradition but subject it to radical reinterpretation. Offensive material thereby becomes innocuous, or on occasion an actual affirmation of the very view of history and the nature of the world on which criticism of the poets was originally based. Most such reinterpretations are either allegorical or rhetorical in character. Thus Homer's unedifying brawl (*Iliad* 21) between gods friendly and hostile to the Trojans becomes an allegory of the perpetual conflict between the elements and the qualities they represent (the heat of fire pitted against the dampness of water, etc.);[1] and the rhetoric of the *Phaedrus* transforms (by implication) poetic fantasies of travel by winged chariot into metaphors for the mobility, self-generating energy, and exalted origin and destiny of the soul.

Rhetoric and allegorical hermeneutics are usually thought of as distinct critical modes.[2] Both, however, are based on the same fundamental view of the separability of expression from meaning; and one type of allegory is, of course, ultimately recognized as a standard rhetorical "figure of thought." Both involve *hermēneia,* a term applicable to the activity of anyone who plays Hermes' role of intermediary in the transmission of a message, and so equally appropriate whether the author's meaning is presented in rhetorical or allegorical guise. The main difference is that, with the allegorical text, what is meant must be ascertained through a process of total substitution—often of something totally different from what is said. A rhetorician's meaning, on the other hand, is usually arrived at through reduction or abstraction or a natural process of association. In the hymns and encomia called for by Plato, gods and heroes are not covert references to the physical elements of the universe or abstractions such as "thought" (Zeus) or "technology"

(Athena), but simply exemplary possessors of power, beauty, goodness, or whatever other quality is associated with a given mythical figure, divine or human.[3] When the rhetorically transmitted meaning is not a simple extension of the meaning a text would have if it were put forward in a perfectly straightforward, non-rhetorical way, it can easily be supplied from textual context or referential situation. If it cannot, this is a sign that the text has failed as rhetoric. Allegory, on the other hand, is not assumed to be the less successful for requiring a sophisticated retranslation (also called *hermēneia*) into its original form before it can be understood.

In semiological terms, allegory and rhetoric both involve an overcoding, and so entail a two-stage process of decoding: first, in order to arrive at the meaning a set of verbal signifiers would have if used in the way normal language uses them; and, then, to arrive at the rhetorical or allegorical significance attached to these meanings.[4] The difference is that the key to the rhetorical overcode is already in the possession of the audience, or so easily supplied that the recipient of the message is not prevented from responding immediately to items doubly coded in this fashion—sometimes even more readily than he would to items singly coded. The allegorical key, on the other hand, may require effort to discover. Zeus as a coding for a supremely just and powerful wielder of authority injects the latter meaning into most contexts just as, or more, effectively than an uncoded presentation would, the authority "figure" being readily understood for what he is. Zeus as a coding for the element air must wait for the ingenuity of a Diogenes of Apollonia (64 A 8) before its existence is even suspected. Perhaps, as the traditional definition of allegory as extended metaphor suggests, the two modes should be located at different points on a single scale. Rhetorical metaphors easily expand along this scale into allegories (ceasing to be rhetorical if the result is obscurity, or an obsession with metaphor for its own sake). Allegories, as they become more transparent or are provided with an explicit key, take their place among rhetorical devices.

The availability of rhetoric and allegory as alternative and closely related ways of reconciling philosophical content with traditional ways of saying things may well have been recognized by

Plato. His suggestion (*Rep.* 10.607a3–4) that poets anxious for a chance to exercise their talents in the ideal state avail themselves of the rhetorical alternative (hymns and encomia) occurs in the same work as does his rejection of the other possibility. (Cf. *Rep.* 3.378d3–e1: allegorical meanings [*hyponoiai*] are too rarely understood for their presence to be of any relevance to the acceptability of a piece of poetry.) Plato's contemporary Antisthenes also seems to have been familiar with both alternatives. He offers the clearest early fourth-century echo (or is it anticipation?)[5] of the Platonic view of rhetoric when he turns Homer's Odysseus, the man "of many devices" (*polytropos*), into the man "of many tropes." The *tropoi* of the epithet are, according to Antisthenes (fr. 51 Caizzi), the different ways in which Odysseus says the same thing, depending on the character of his addressees. Elsewhere (fr. 58), Homer is presented as an allegorist composing regularly on two levels: the first is that of opinion (the apparent meaning of the allegory), and the second is that of truth (its real meaning, or *hyponoia*). It is not known whether Antisthenes would have used the same truth–opinion contrast in analyzing Odyssean *tropoi,* but the parallel between his conceptions of allegory and rhetoric is clear enough.

The connection of the two modes is of considerable consequence for the history of rhetoric, since allegorizing reinterpretation of the poetic tradition—like the rationalizing rewriting first attested in Stesichorus—is almost as old as the criticism that provoked it. It is associated with the name of Theagenes of Rhegium; and Theagenes, like Xenophanes and Stesichorus, lived in the sixth century.[6] If the combination of rhetoric and allegory found in Antisthenes is as easy and natural as it seemed to his contemporaries, one might expect both techniques to make their appearance in Greek discussions of poetry at approximately the same time. What the evidence from the period between Theagenes and Antisthenes actually suggests, however, is that allegory was somewhat the earlier of the two.

Prodicus of Ceos, a contemporary of Antisthenes' master Socrates, offers fairly clear examples of both modes. In tracing the origin of religion to the personification and subsequent deification of those things that most benefited the life of the human race (wine personified as Dionysus, grain as Demeter, etc.), Prodicus adopts an implicitly allegorical view of mythological narrative, and the most famous of all his writings made conscious use of allegory for rhetorical purposes. This piece (84B1) develops the contrast between a life of self-indulgence and a life of discipline and achievement in the form of a debate between two female figures, Virtue and Pleasure, who confront the hero Heracles at a crossroads and describe what awaits him if he follows one path rather than another at the symbolic parting of the ways to which he has come. Personifications of things, processes, and forces are, of course, a standard feature of Greek poetry at least from the time of Hesiod, but personifications usually occur in contexts where genealogy or narrative is either the most natural or the only means at the poet's disposal for conveying his meaning (see chapter 3, n. 4). What sets Prodicus's Choice of Heracles apart from earlier texts as a rhetorical allegory is the superfluousness—at one level—of his personifications. They are there simply to make more vivid and memorable an argument all of whose phases would be perfectly clear without them. The same cannot be said of, say, the phases through which, in Hesiod's *Theogony,* world history must pass in order to move from the reign of elemental forces of nature (the Sea, Sky, Stars, Wind, Hurricane, and Volcano of 233 ff.) to that of Zeus and the Olympians.

Going back a generation or two from Prodicus, to the thinker who first drew the radical distinction between truth and opinion on which Antisthenes based his view of Odysseus's many *tropoi,* one finds in the proem of Parmenides a profusion of motifs and images from poetic accounts of heroic voyages used to describe a philosophical voyage to, or along, the Way of Truth. Since these motifs, like everything the poets say, are a part of the Way of Seeming, and that Way, according to Parmenides, has nothing to do with Truth, their presence in a philosophical text can only be justified as rhetorical *amplificatio.* They serve to underline the uniqueness and supreme importance of the philosopher's quest.

A slightly later figure, Protagoras, is also the author of a celebrated piece of rhetorical myth—if the general consensus of modern scholarship is right in assuming that *Protagoras* 320c8–22d5 is a reasonably accurate report of the Sophist's teaching rather than an invention of Plato. In that passage the process of social conditioning by which all men in a given society are forced to acquire the minimum of civic virtue necessary for society to function effectively is explained or allegorized as Zeus's gift to mankind of reverence and justice, the two constituents of the "civic" art (*politikē technē*); and the special education by which intellectual and technological skills are passed on is similarly allegorized as Prometheus's distribution of the "craftsmanly" art (*demiourgikē technē*) unequally among different members of the species. The combination of the civic and craftsmanly art is to human beings what Epimetheus's gift (described earlier in the myth) of swiftness, strength, fecundity, or protective fur and skins was to various animals: a necessary survival mechanism for the species. As in Prodicus, the meaning of the rhetorical myth is developed separately—and at considerable length—in the completely literal, non-rhetorical discourse that follows it (322e–28d).

Nothing comparable survives from writers earlier than Parmenides and Protagoras.[7] The earliest clear samples of allegorical narrative used rhetorically are thus later, by at least a generation, than allegorical interpretation itself (Theagenes) or rationalized and "corrected" mythological narrative (Stesichorus). And it is worth noting that the examples that can be cited are almost all ascribed to figures linked directly or indirectly to the Socratic tradition: Socrates' spiritual "father" Parmenides (cf. *Theaetetus* 183e–84a), his pupils Antisthenes and Plato, the Sophist (Prodicus) most closely associated with him by his contemporaries, and (on occasion, at any rate) the Platonic Socrates himself (represented [*Phaedo* 61b3–7] as occupying his time in prison by putting examples of a related form of discourse, the Aesopic *ainos*, into verse).[8]

Protagoras, of course, has no such Socratic affinities; but it is Plato who attributes the *Protagoras* myth to him, and the general consensus in favor of this attribution is not necessarily correct. Some scholars have drawn attention, with good reason, to elements in the myth that sound more Platonic than Protagorean.[9] The classification of all arts as either civic or craftsmanly is a typically Platonic diaeresis, and one based on a typically Socratic analogy drawn from the realm of the useful arts and crafts. A reference, injected irrelevantly into the course of the myth, to belief in the gods as yet another trait that distinguishes human beings from animals (322a3–5) is hard to square with Protagoras's self-proclaimed agnosticism (B4). The notion that justice and reverence come from Zeus, and so have what is in some sense a higher origin than the technology received from Prometheus, suggests a contempt for banausic skills which is well attested for Plato but not for Protagoras. Moreover, it introduces fundamental difficulties into the whole account. The cooperative, social stage of human existence referred to must postdate Zeus's gift of justice and reverence (322d1–5); yet that stage is already presupposed in earlier references (322a5–8, 322c5–7) to the development of language and the division of labor between specialists in the various craftsmanly skills. Finally, it is possible to point to fairly close parallels in fifth-century texts to all the essential ideas contained in the myth— except the idea of presenting them in mythical guise.[10] Prometheus appears as the bestower of a saving technology in the *Prometheus Bound,* and in a context that is at least partially allegorical; but the allegory centers around Prometheus's punishment by Zeus, not his activity as a bringer of culture. And Prometheus is first explicitly equated with human inventiveness and intelligence (*nous*) in a fragment of the comic poet Plato (136 Kock) which may well postdate the death of Protagoras.[11]

It would probably be going too far on the basis of such evidence to suggest that Plato simply invented the myth he transmits, thereby supplying what would strike his fourth-century readers as an appropriately archaic cast for the ideas of an earlier thinker. But false "archaism" of this sort may well have been a significant consideration, leading him to turn a Sophistic piece of rationalized mythology into an original mythological allegory. What are presented in his text as personifications of human forethought (Prometheus), fire-based technology (Hephaestus), and craftsmanly intelligence (Athena) may have been in his Protagorean original the divine inventors (or supposed inventors) of the various arts, adduced in passing to support the writer's basic contention. "A further indication," he might have argued, "of the universality of the civic skill is that, whereas other craftsmen have each of them his own patron god (Prometheus, Hephaestus, Athena) from whose teaching their skill is thought to derive, no one ventures to say whence right and reverence came—only that they are somehow 'from Zeus'" (cf. Soph., *Antigone* 450–57, on the sources of "unwritten" law).

If secure instances of rhetorical re-use of allegorized mythology are considerably later than allegorical interpretation itself, explicit appeal to the view of discourse underlying such use is later still. It is first attested in the year 405 B.C., at the point in Aristophanes' *Frogs* where Aeschylus is finally allowed to reply to the charge that his tragedies are long-winded, bombastic, implausible, and concerned with things remote from everyday affairs (by contrast with those of Euripides, which are clear, relevant, and full of argumentational cleverness and practical advice).[12] The counterargument Aeschylus presents stresses the powerful incitement to patriotic virtue that his plays provide through their depiction of heroic exemplars (1021–22, 1040–42). Their style may be inflated but is an appropriate dress for their content: verbalizations of mighty thoughts and sentiments (1059: *megalōn gnōmōn kai dianoiōn rhēmata*) must be larger than life, like the clothes worn by demigods. Taken together, the two ideas bring the passage fairly close to those from later antiquity,[13] in which the grand narrative manner is presented and justified as an illustration of military and political virtues in action, couched in appropriately particular terms and with the elaboration necessary to attract and hold people's attention—primitive audiences, and all audiences made up of ordinary people, being incapable of responding to any other sort of exhortation to virtue.

Aeschylus's position, however, is only introduced by way of a response to Euripides' attack; and this order of presentation— first Euripides' critique, then Aeschylus's reply—may well correspond to the order of development in the intellectual history of the fifth century. Aeschylus looks forward at this point to the rhetorical criticism of a later day, whereas Euripides echoes what was probably a well-established Sophistic tradition that criticizes poets for being unedifying, inconsistent, implausible, or outright mis-taken—for failing, in other words, to perform their traditional informative and educational function in an acceptable manner. Protagoras thus takes Homer to task (B III 3) for commanding the Muse to sing at the opening of the *Iliad* rather than, presumably, requesting her, as the deference due a deity would require. The criticism Plato has Protagoras make of Simonides at *Protagoras* 339a6–d9 is of the same character. The poet is convicted of saying in consecutive stanzas of his poem to Scopas, first that excellence is "hard to come by," and then—in apparent contradiction to this—that the sage Pittacus was wrong in saying that excellence is "hard to possess." Protagoras's complaint is answered in very much the same spirit when, later in the dialogue, his fellow Sophist Prodicus is made to go along with two points in Socrates' counterinterpreta-tion of the poem. Socrates suggests, first, that Protagoras was wrong to assume that the words here translated as "come by" and "possess" have the same meaning (339b3–d5); then, that in one of the two stanzas Simonides must have given to the phrase "hard to possess" the meaning it had in his own Cean dialect, where "hard" is synonymous with "bad" (341a5–41d1).

We are not told how Protagoras himself proposed to solve the difficulty, and the whole discussion, insofar as it has to do with the interpretation of this particular poem, may be Plato's invention. But both the fault detected and the solutions endorsed by Prodicus are suggestive of a type of early poetic exegesis familiar to Aristotle and extensively documented both in his *Homeric Problems* (frs. 142–79 Rose) and in the twenty-fifth chapter of his *Poetics*. The subject of the latter passage is the various "errors" detected in poetry by earlier critics, most of whom, it is generally agreed, must have been Sophists.[14] The errors alleged involve inaccuracies, improbabilities (that Oedipus would never have inquired into the circumstances of Laius's death at the time; that the Achaeans would continue to hold back while Achilles pursues Hector alone in *Iliad* 22), things that set a bad example (heroes ordering their drinks mixed stronger [*Iliad* 9.203]), or inconsistencies (the state-ment [*Iliad* 10.1] that the whole world, men and gods alike, was asleep, followed ten lines later by reference to the sound of pipes and flutes in the Trojan camp). And the proposed answers to these criticisms follow generally "Prodicean" lines when they suggest that a rare or dialectal word has been misunderstood, or the wrong sense given to an ambiguous one, or a phrase mispunctuated or wrongly accented, or a false charge of historical inaccuracy made because of the critic's own ignorance of historical evidence corroborating the poet's version of an episode.

It is true that other and quite different lines of reply are also suggested by Aristotle. He says that inaccuracies and unlikelihoods can be justified because they are in accord with an audience's view of what happened or should happen (and so conducive to the success of the piece as mimesis); or that they may be small or inconspicuous parts of an otherwise acceptable whole; or that they are metaphorically rather than literally true; or that they are less noticeable because embedded in a causal sequence that leads the audience to make a fallacious inference (*paralogismos*) of events from their normal and expected consequences; or that they are conducive to the *telos* of the art in question, which is to make a passage more striking and effective (*ekplēktikon*). All these answers, however, are closely bound up with characteristically Aristotelian preoccupations (mimesis, metaphor [cf. *Rhet.* 3.2–4], the unity and wholeness of a work of art, logical fallacy and the various forms it may take, characterization of an art by reference to its *telos*). They also provide Aristotle with effective means for defending those parts of a poet's work that are wrong by other criteria but do not constitute a fault "in terms of the art itself" (*pros autēn tēn technēn; autēs tēs poietikēs . . . kath' eautēn:* cf. *Poet.* 25.1460b13–31). Aristotle compares these "faults" to such plausible untruths as an artist's "successful" representation of a horse with both right hooves advanced or a doe with horns. If the things actually existed, they might be expected to appear as the artist depicts them.

What are here described as characteristically Aristotelian contributions to the criticism of the poets are also characteristically rhetorical ones. They do not deny that accuracy, verisimilitude, logic, and moral acceptability are all qualities that might be legitimately demanded of a poet just as they are of a philosopher or historian. But the focus of their criticism is elsewhere—not on the intrinsic truth or value of what is said, but on its effectiveness as a means of getting across the content of a particular work of art and of realizing its mimetic goals. And similar criteria of communicational effectiveness guide the rhetorician whenever he produces an analysis or defense of a piece of oratorical prose.

The typically Aristotelian character of these "rhetorical" considerations and the necessary role they play in his own defense of poetry suggest that they were original with him, not taken over from some extensive earlier body of rhetorically oriented criticism. Such criticism was, to judge from the "Aeschylean" samples quoted from Aristophanes, fairly spare and rudimentary in character. And this conclusion is supported by the fact that, though justification of poetry in rhetorical terms is essential to Aristophanes' defense of Aeschylus, it is embedded, just as its more sophisticated Aristotelian counterparts are, in a larger critical context based on totally different principles. In that context, the informative role of the poet is the crucial thing, just as it had been in Euripides' attack. Thus in reply to the charge that the information he supplies is irrelevant and out of date, Aeschylus points out (*Frogs* 1026 ff.) how poets have, from time immemorial, been a source of knowledge pertaining to religious rites, purifications, medicine, divination, agriculture, times for sowing and planting, animal husbandry, military weapons and tactics, and, finally, "virtue."

Only the last item on the list is in line with the rhetorical defense of his own work that Aeschylus offers at 1021–22, 1041–42, and 1059; and even that defense shows signs of having borrowed and modified an assessment carried out originally on different, arhetorical principles. Gorgias had spoken of the *Seven against Thebes* as a play "full of Ares" (B24), probably referring to the impression of accuracy and immediacy with which it brings home to the spectator the phenomenon of war in all its aspects. This would, at any rate, be in line with his remarks elsewhere about the willing suspension of disbelief (B23) and total identification with the protagonists (*Helen* 9) that characterizes the audience at a dramatic performance. Aristophanes has Aeschylus use the same phrase (1021), but he turns Gorgias's play full of war into a play full of martial spirit: a piece of *ēthos*-based persuasion so effective that "everyone who saw it could hardly wait to enlist" (1022). The result is to import into the play a specific rhetorical message that is much less evident in Aeschylus's text—and, one suspects, in most early reactions to the play—than either the vividness of the evocation of the sights and sounds and terrors of a city under siege, or the direct information conveyed, through Eteocles' speeches and exchanges with the chorus, of the problems created by the simultaneous presence of a hostile army outside the walls and quarreling leaders and a hysterical population within. (One could hardly imagine a less effective piece of recruiting propaganda.)[15]

Besides antedating the rhetorical view of traditional poetry, the "modernist" critique may also have been a prerequisite for it. As noted earlier, the rationalizing tradition to which the Sophistic belongs was concerned with rewriting history and mythology to meet the demands of logic, empirical observation, and Ionian "science." To those involved in it the process doubtless seemed a single, unified effort to purge traditional lore of the fabrications with which poetic fancy had encumbered it. From a later, rhetorical perspective it can be seen as a movement proceeding in parallel fashion on the levels of both style and content. The result was, on one level, a defictionalized version of the content of the tradition—a version from which illogicalities and inconsistencies and fantastic elements had been removed. Such was the picture of the past produced by the Ionian logographers. But this version was also as stylistically plain as it was intellectually straightforward: a series of simple chronicles painfully devoid of any kind of figurative language or artistic molding of the narrative.

The ideal that lies behind Sophistic criticism of the poets is similarly twofold—a "straight speaking," to use the Protagorean term (*orthoepeia*: A26), which probably includes both a way of relaying pieces of information which is straightforward (not crooked or false) and a style that contains no deviation from the norm (of idiom, logic, grammar, or literal correctness).[16] The effort to identify a set of fully understandable, consistent, unambiguous linguistic usages and locate them at the core of Greek vocabulary, syntax, and style goes hand in hand with the effort to isolate a core of truth within the typical fabric of poetic invention—a plausible account, based partially on inference and reconstruction, of the actual events that might have served poets as a starting point for their fanciful elaborations. The transformation of style that results from this effort is most conspicuous in the narrative manner of Euripides, the transformation of content in the accounts of the logographers.[17] But both derive ultimately from the same source.

Once isolated in this fashion, a core of plain truth could easily become a core of meaning surrounded by an accretion of rhetorical techniques deployed for its more effective transmission, whether through prose or verse. Its stylistic counterpart—a core of plain statement—could serve as a nucleus around which, by similar processes of accretion, contrasting rhetorical manners of presentation could be created. But before the process of isolation had created an actual body of texts, it would have been, if not impossible, at least difficult to arrive at the notion of the essential, "non-rhetorical" core of a piece of discourse through a purely mental effort at abstraction. The emperor had to be stripped of his clothes before it could occur to anyone that he had been wearing them.

Until this happened, allegorical interpreters of the poets were doubtless as blind as anyone else to the rhetorical potentialities of indirect, veiled utterance; and what they contributed to the new discipline did not go beyond the general idea of the possibility of a gap between what texts say and what they mean, or a few specific pieces of allegorized myth that could be put to rhetorical use. In the later proliferation of rhetorical techniques, allegory was destined to take its place simply as one among many. It was an isolated remnant of an earlier defense of poetry incorporated into the larger, more secure structure erected for that purpose in the fourth century and after.

The purposes this structure of rhetorical analysis and theory served were, of course, much more extensive than the defense of poetry. The Sophists in particular are usually assumed to have aimed at nothing less than a wholesale modification and expansion of the repertory of poetic distortion and deception, taking it over and adapting it, in an argumentative context, to the very sort of inaccurate, immoral, or illogical discourse they had criticized in their predecessors. This view, however, derives ultimately from one strand in the Platonic and Aristotelian analysis (see chapter 1) of the uses and abuses of "protorhetoric." It is a view very difficult to square with what survives of the actual writings of the Sophists and their fifth-century contemporaries. The evidence—to be examined in the following two chapters—suggests that, in the realm of argumentation as well as that of historical and mythological narrative, their contribution to the development of rhetoric continued to be as indirect as it was crucial. Aristophanes may provide, in the last analysis, a better guide to the character of the period than either Plato or Aristotle. It is Euripides, the pupil of the Sophists, who in the decisive weighing of words and assessing of achievements that closes the *Frogs* gives perfectly clear and straightforward (if silly) advice to his fellow citizens (1427–29, 1437–50); and it is Aeschylus, soon to be resuscitated to help Athens face her future, who speaks rhetorically, in transparent metaphors (1431–32) and portentous riddles (1463–68).[18]

THE LATE
FIFTH
CENTURY

Five

Technē and Text

A crucial stumbling block in the way of any theory that places the origins and first flowering of rhetoric in late fifth-century Athens is the overall character of the Attic prose which survives from that period. It is hard to imagine an idiom or a style less calculated to please or move an audience, or to make a message more acceptable and more understandable, than those which appear time and again in the orations of Antiphon, the speeches of Thucydides' history, and the largely anonymous or fragmentary remains of the prose of their contemporaries. Gorgias's notorious funeral oration (82 B 6) is an extreme case, but not an isolated one:

What did these men lack that men should have?
And what did they have that men should lack?
May what I say be what I sought to say,
and what I sought to say what I ought to say—
  free from the wrath of gods,
  far from the envy of men.
They had the virtue that is instilled by gods,
and the mortality that is inborn in men—
  judging the gentleness of sacrifice better than the harshness of
    demanding one's due,

far better soundness of spirit than the letter of the law—
thinking duty in duty's place and time the most divine and
   universal of laws
   whether in things done or not done,
   said or left unsaid;
schooling themselves into what was most needed:
   might of hand and rightness of plan,
   thinking through the one
   and acting out the other;
succorers of the unfairly unfortunate,
punishers of the unfairly fortunate;
   assertive when advantage called,
   yielding when propriety forbade;
   restraining hastiness of hand
      with prudence of plan;
   confronting outrage with outrage,
      orderliness with order;
   fearless in the face of the fearless,
   feared themselves in the midst of things to be feared;
in testimony to which they raised trophies over their enemies:
   for themselves, dedications;
   for Zeus, consecrations;
strangers neither to the fire of battle in the blood,
   nor chaste loves,
   nor armor-clad strife,
   nor beauty-loving peace,
showing reverence to the gods through justice,
   devotion to parents through care,
   justice to fellow-countrymen through fairness
   respect to friends through faith.
Dead though they be, our longing for them dies not;
but deathless in bodies not deathless, it lives, though they live not.

One inevitably wonders "how such a style can have moved to
transports of delight men who lived among the works of Pheidias
and Iktinos, who knew the prose of Herodotus, and whose ears
were familiar with Homer, with Aeschylus and with Sophocles"; or
even, "how it was that Gorgias . . . was able 'to get away with it.'"[1]
And Gorgias's prose shares with that of his Athenian contempo-

raries a whole series of strikingly "arhetorical" qualities. One finds everywhere a kind of stiff formality—evident, for example, in the restrained use made of colloquial particles; harshness to the ear stemming from neglect of the rules of euphony that ensure a smooth, easy flow of sound from word to word (cf. Dionysius of Halicarnassus, *De comp. verb.* 22); balanced echoing sentence structure—recognizable even when, as in Thucydides, imbalances and incongruities are frequently injected to disguise its presence; a grammar and syntax that is, by Herodotean or Platonic standards, strikingly regular, precise, and complex; compressed density of ideas and argumentation (the quality, attributed by Cicero to the *antiquissimi* among Greek orators [*De or.* 2.92] of being *sententiis magis quam verbis abundantes*); the absence of any attempt to give *ēthos* to what is said by making it suggest the character of the person or class of person who is saying it; and a tendency toward abstract modes of expression combined with an emphasis on what is of general applicability and permanent significance at the expense of the particular, the merely picturesque and curious, or what is of only passing relevance. (Contrast Thucydides' rigidly selective view of what is worth inclusion in his history with Herodotus's apparent willingness to include anything that caught his fancy at the moment of narration; or, in oratory, contrast the brief, sketchy way past action is presented by Antiphon with the elaborate mimetic realization it receives in Demosthenes.)

It is just possible that a burgeoning art of rhetoric would use, and misuse, echo and balance—in an effort to recover some of the impressiveness that was lost when poetic meter and poetic diction were abandoned. But it is difficult to see why it would have cultivated the other qualities enumerated: formality, harshness, syntactical regularity, grammatical precision, compactness, neglect of *ēthos,* abstractness, and generality. Many of these qualities suggest, rather, the operation of the sort of intellectualism discussed in the preceding chapter. Attic prose of this period is a prose of information and ideas: its aim is to free syntax of extravagance and irregularity; it is couched in the general, abstract terms needed for its sweeping reorganization of inherited views; it is given to treating considerations dictated by euphony with disdain, and it is inclined to regard intrusions of the colloquial with actual suspicion.

This prose is removed in one further way from anything ordinarily thought of as rhetorical: it is obviously a written prose, composed to be studied and deciphered by the eye as well as heard by the ear.[2] Compactness, precision, regularity, and complexity are all more effective in a work composed for perusal at leisure than in one improvised for oral performance, and the syntactical features mentioned are probably essential components of that exactness (*akribeia*) regularly seen (Arist., *Rhet.* 3.12 1413b8–9) as characteristic of written rather than oral discourse. By the same token, harshness to the ear, formal stiffness, and lack of attention to euphony are more likely to be excused by a reader than by an audience.

Inconceivable apart from the use of writing, the typical late fifth-century text must nevertheless reflect, at some level, an effort to meet the needs of oral delivery as well. It is obvious that the speeches of Antiphon and Thucydides are not simply "reference and consultation" texts, written compendia of information for those who might have occasion to refer to them, or expert opinion recorded for the benefit of those who might not be able to consult an expert in person. Such "reference" texts were produced in some abundance during the period, but they are composed, almost without exception, in Ionic rather than Attic, and in a style that shows none of the "Attic" qualities enumerated except compactness—the result of their authors' inclination to stay as close as possible to strict circumstantiality in narration.

Attic literature of the period is equally poor in true "reading" texts—texts intended to provide their users with the same things for which one would go to a poetic recitation or a Sophistic epideixis: entertainment (*terpsis*) or general enlightenment and education (*paideia*). The earliest "reading" texts were probably anthologies culled from "performance" texts such as those used by the Homeric rhapsodes or Herodotus as a basis for professional recitals. Any reading texts that did not originate in this way are likely to have been, once again, Ionic rather than Attic. Obvious possibilities are the works of Ion of Chios and Stesimbrotos of

Thasos—gossipy compilations about the lives of leading personalities of the writers' own generation and the one immediately preceding. There is no trace in fifth-century Attic writing of texts that would have had a comparable appeal to a reading public.

The public that writers in Attic had in mind seems to have been rather different: a public of speakers, or prospective speakers, rather than of readers or researchers. And the typical Attic text gives the impression of having been composed for "practice and demonstration." It is a model piece devoted to the sort of subject likely to come up for repeated discussion in political, judicial, or epideictic oratory and designed to be useful in as wide a variety of such situations as possible. The best-known texts of this sort still extant are the twelve which are grouped by fours into the *Tetralogies* of Antiphon, and the four which develop first a relativistic and then an antirelativistic argument as to the nature of the good, the noble, the just, and the true in the so-called *Twofold Arguments (Dissoi Logoi)*, composed about 400 B.C. We know, however, that similar texts were also produced by Antiphon's contemporary Gorgias. Cicero refers to "discussions of important and recurring themes" (*rerum illustrium disputationes*) in the form of "presentations, each devoted to a single topic, of advantages and disadvantages" (*singularum rerum laudes vituperationesque: Brutus* 47 = B VII 26). Such commonplaces were written down (Cicero, *Brutus* 47) and distributed to students to memorize (Arist., *Soph. El.* 33 183b38–39).

It would be easy for such practice and demonstration texts to become "display" texts as well, pieces designed to show off the master's skill to admiring amateurs as well as illustrate its workings to prospective professionals. Of the two complete works of Gorgias that survive, the *Helen* or "Apology" for Helen and the *Defense of Palamedes,* the former probably belongs to this category. But its epideictic function has not been allowed to interfere with its pedagogical one. In reviewing the possible reasons that might account for Helen's disastrous elopement with Paris—physical constraint, the will of the gods, amorous infatuation, or the persuasive power of speech—Gorgias argues that any or all of them would have been sufficient to put Helen in a position where she could not fairly be held accountable for her actions. His text contains, in addition, a largely irrelevant introduction and a bravura digression on the various forms persuasive speech may take; but in substance it is an illustration of what later rhetoricians (for example, Quint. 7.41) would call the *status qualitativus*. This *status*, or case category, exists when the facts involved and their legality or morality are not in dispute, but rather the "quality" of the transgression committed: willing or unwilling, linked or not linked to extenuating circumstances. In similar fashion, though with much less irrelevant display, Palamedes' defense against the charge of having conspired to betray the Greek camp at Troy to the enemy provides a model for the *status coniecturalis*—the type of argument concerned with determining what actually occurred (cf. Cicero, *De inv.* 1.8.10). More particularly, it is a study of the role of such a *status* of circumstantial evidence and plausible reconstruction of motives, conducted through a close examination of the inadequacies of both insofar as they might be expected to figure in the prosecution of Palamedes.

It is inconceivable that either discourse was intended to serve in its entirety as a model of how to plead a single case. Gorgias adduces so many reasons for absolving Helen of responsibility, so many lacunae and possibilities of opposite interpretation in the circumstantial evidence against Palamedes, and so many difficulties of establishing a plausible motive for what Palamedes is accused of doing, that he provides appropriate grounds for dismissing such cases in almost any situation in which they might arise, not simply in the two under discussion.[3] And this is, one suspects, precisely Gorgias's intention. There is to be, so far as possible, no case to which some of his arguments would *not* apply, and, as a consequence, no case to which all of them *would* apply. The particular situation, when it arises, will determine which of the arguments presented would be of actual use to the pupil who memorized the sample piece.

Also determined by the particular situation, or the abilities of the particular pupil, would be the amount of elaboration and expansion that oral presentation brought to a written text. The Sophist Prodicus, we are told (Arist., *Rhet.* 3.14 1415b15–17), was in the habit of enlivening his three-drachma lecture with extracts from his forty-drachma lecture whenever he saw that the attention of the audience was wandering; and if either version was available in written form it was doubtless the three-drachma one. This is a natural inference from the way Xenophon has Socrates introduce his retelling of the famous Prodicean story of Heracles at the crossroads (*Mem.* 2.1.21 ff.).

Three versions are implied in Xenophon's account: (1) a written piece (*syngramma*) which Prodicus "exhibits" (or "is exhibited" [*epideiknytai*] by Prodicus) to large numbers of people; (2) Socrates' own imperfect presentation "from memory"; and (3) the way Prodicus himself was in the habit of setting forth the story when he delivered it orally: "in much finer language" (*rhēmasi megaleioterois*) than any found in Socrates' approximation. Many scholars have been reluctant to take Xenophon's second version at face value: Socrates' presentation, they feel, is so polished that he must be reproducing the *syngramma* more or less verbatim. An alternative possibility is that Socrates' denigration of his own efforts is ironic, and that Xenophon is giving an imitation (or parody) of what he conceived to be the Prodicean oral manner, basing himself on a *syngramma* that left ample room for such reformulations. But in any case the passage implies a considerable difference between the written piece of the first version and the oral presentation or *epideixis* of the third version. The latter must have involved much more than a mere reading aloud with appropriate gestures and intonations.

A ten-page demonstration text in Antiphon's *Tetralogies*—two speeches for the prosecution and two for the defense, composed as if for the trial of a boy who has accidentally killed a fellow athlete with a javelin—may be regarded as another three-drachma piece, the forty-drachma version being on the scale of the longer discussion Pericles and Protagoras are said to have had on a similar case, devoting a whole day (Plutarch, *Pericles* 36) of debate to the question of how the incident should be described and defined, and where responsibility placed: with the victim, or the thrower of the javelin, or the javelin itself. The discussion may have inspired the Antiphontic demonstration piece, or vice versa; or the two may have been completely independent of each other. Once again, however, the striking difference in scale—and so, presumably, in the range and character of the arguments used—is indicative of a very wide gap between oral performance and written model.

Not all the Attic texts surviving from the late fifth century are demonstrably practice pieces of this sort, and it would be risky to maintain that the "Attic" qualities of style discussed earlier could be found *only* in such texts. But those qualities are at home there to an extent they would not be in a reading, reference, or performance text. If formality, harshness, syntactical precision, and complexity are natural or excusable in prose designed for reading, their presence is even more to be expected in a work meant for prolonged study rather than casual perusal or occasional consultation. And echoing sound effects can just as easily be a mnemonic device as the result of initial efforts to create for prose an aural impressiveness comparable to what is found in poetry. Ask anyone who heard or read the piece at the time of delivery to recall as much as he can remember of John F. Kennedy's inaugural address, and he is likely to come up with two outrageous "Gorgianisms":

> Let us never negotiate from fear,
> but let us never fear to negotiate.

> Ask not what your country can do for you,
> but what you can do for your country.

A whole speech composed, like Gorgias's Funeral Oration, of such jingles might well tax the patience of listeners who "knew the prose" of Churchill, and whose "ears were familiar" with Shakespeare and Shaw. But it might also be, once committed to writing, a brilliant piece of pedagogical compression—a single paragraph packed with enough material to keep a student well supplied for an entire performance or series of performances in the real world of ceremonial eloquence.[4] Here, as elsewhere in fifth-century prose, compactness arises from the desire to compress into easily memorized and mastered compass as much model material as possible. Like the *Helen*, only more so, the result is a "toy" (*paignion*: cf. 21), but at the same time—also like the *Helen* in this respect—an educational toy. (Even a certain element of self-parody is not excluded. Gorgias is on record as having appreciated the value of humor in countering the serious allegations of an opponent,[5] and he may have been equally aware of the usefulness of parody and pastiche as a means for focusing students' attention and making their memories more retentive.) It would follow, if this suggestion is correct, that Gorgias's famous oral improvisations on any theme his audience cared to propose (see 82 A 1a) need not have been conspicuous for their use of the figures—rhyme, short balancing phrases, close syntactical parallelism—which were later known as Gorgianic. In fact, the earliest writer to associate those figures with Gorgias is the historian Timaeus (third century B.C.).[6] They could have been simply a prominent feature of Gorgias's written demonstration pieces that became linked with his name only when the memory of the oral performances on which his reputation was chiefly based had largely disappeared.[7]

The remaining "Attic" qualities point even more clearly to the demands of the practice and demonstration text. *Ethos* is most easily dispensed with when it is irrelevant—as in a work designed to serve as a basis for oral presentations by many different speakers; and abstractness and generality are likely to be most pervasive when concentration on the particular is not simply irrelevant but counterproductive—a sure way to decrease the paradigmatic usefulness of what is being said. Finally, the difference between Attica and Ionia falls into place once one realizes that the conditions that favored the production of practice and demonstration texts existed in Attica to a degree that they did not in Ionia, and were the very conditions that would tend to inhibit the production of any other type of written prose.

The busy sessions of courts and assemblies, and the crowded halls dedicated to Sophistic or eristic debate were an inseparable and characteristic part of Athenian life in the fifth century. The neophyte confronted by choice or necessity with the prospect of taking part in such sessions would be an eager user of any text that could select and compress what was likely to prove of recurring practical value in the performances of recognized masters and preserve it in isolation from what was less valuable. Such texts would be less unwieldy to handle than verbatim transcripts, less trouble to master, and less expensive to buy.

But the very frequency of the occasions on which such written models could prove useful would have tended to discourage the production of reference or reading texts. Those occasions were, as abundant testimony from the time makes clear, an essential part of Athens' role as the one great emporium, central clearing house, and high court and council chamber (*prytaneion*) for everything that was said or thought in Greece.[8] Anyone with political or intellectual ambitions who wished to inform himself on the latest scientific theories and discoveries, or to be entertained by the latest historical or Sophistic epideixis, or to inform or entertain others in the same way with the results of his own intellectual activities, had simply to take a brief stroll down to the agora, or keep himself posted on happenings in the houses of the leading patrons of artistic and intellectual endeavor. For he could be fairly certain that sooner or later everyone in the Greek community worth hearing or talking to would turn up in one place or the other.

This "metropolitan" culture stands in sharp contrast to the "cosmopolitan" culture of the Ionian intellectual community in the same period and during the course of the preceding century. Ionian intellectuals were widely scattered through the islands and coasts of the Aegean and had limited opportunities for coming together for the exchange of ideas. If the research or speculation conducted in Miletus or Ephesus was to be made available to prospective users in Teos or Abdera there would have to be texts for consultation and, eventually, reading. It was in places such as those that written texts intended for circulation were probably first produced, during the course of the sixth century, and where they continued to be in most demand—until the advent, in the late fifth century, of the characteristically Attic practice and demonstration text.[9]

This innovation was to have far-reaching effects, for it made popular, probably for the first time, a pedagogic technique that belongs clearly to the repertory of what later came to be called rhetoric. The "protorhetorical" practice and demonstration text is simply, as has often been pointed out, a written version of the exercise (*scholē, meletē*) of Hellenistic and post-Hellenistic times, best known through its Latin outgrowth or equivalent, the *declamatio*. Less often discussed, though more important, is the exact historical relationship between this type of work and what was to emerge in later times as the single most important vehicle of rhetorical instruction, the systematic collection of precepts and analyses.[10] The question is complicated by the fact that the same word (*technē* = Lat. *ars*) can be used to apply both to the systematic, theoretical treatise (Aristotle's *Technē rhētorikē,* for example) and the practical demonstration text—or, since publication in the earliest period was for future users rather than readers, any specimen of an orator's skill that was published rather than composed solely for delivery, whether by oneself or someone else, on a single occasion. Antiphon (B X 7–8), Gorgias (B VII 1), Lysias (B XXIII 9), Theramenes (B XV 3), and Isocrates (B XXIV 14) are all credited with the composition of *technai* which must be, it is generally agreed, model speeches or actual orations designed to serve as models.[11] These are the sort of paradigmatic pieces Isocrates (13.12–13) has in mind when he criticizes protorhetoricians for offering "a fixed *technē* as a model for a process that is creative" (*poiētikou pragmatos tetagmenēn technēn paradeigma*):

> Anyone can see that whatever has to do with writing is rigid and unchangeable and that with speech just the reverse is true. What has been said by someone else can never be useful to a later speaker to the same degree: those considered the most skillful speakers are those whose remarks are original as well as to the point. . . . Freshness, a sense of the occasion and the ability to respond to it must be present to some degree in any successful speech, but once written texts come into being they have no further need of such qualities—sufficient reason for fining rather than paying money to those who offer models of such a sort for imitation (*hoi chrōmenoi tois toioutois paradeigmasin*).

This "Isocratean" meaning is the less frequently attested of the two, but it is one with which even Aristotle was still perfectly familiar. He must have had passages such as this in mind when he spoke of the *technai* Isocrates wrote later in his career (presumably, model pieces such as the *Helen, Busiris, Plataikos,* and *Archidamos*)

81

as belying the orator's earlier denial of the very possibility of any *technē* of speaking (fr. 137 Rose = A V 9). And the balance of the evidence suggests that the less frequent meaning is the earlier—that practice and demonstration texts were, to begin with, the only, or at any rate the most characteristic, and most influential compositions of those teachers whose written *technai* came to be regarded as the beginnings of rhetoric.[12]

Theodectes, a contemporary and, in all probability, associate of Aristotle, is the first author known for certain to have composed a theoretical, analytical *technē* listing and evaluating the various procedures that he felt to be especially appropriate to each of the four "parts"—proem, narrative, proof, and epilogue—normally found in a courtroom speech (fr. 133 Rose). The accounts (A V 16, B II 23) that ascribe a similar arrangement to Corax, the founder of the whole tradition, are both late (see chapter 1) and in disagreement among themselves as to the number of parts (three, four, or seven) and the type of oratory involved (dicanic or symbouleutic). They seem, moreover, to contradict Aristotle's statement (*Rhet.* 2.24 1402a17), apropos of one form of the argument from probability (*eikos*), that "this is what the *technē* of Corax is composed of (*sygkeimenē*)." A *technē* largely or exclusively confined to *eikos* is impossible if Corax dealt with anything but the "proof" section of a speech, where such argumentation usually appeared—and barely possible even in an analysis of proofs.[13]

On the other hand, it is quite easy to see how a whole *technē* could consist of model speeches based on *eikos*: the famous prosecution and defense on a charge of assault and battery referred to at *Phaedrus* 273b3–c4 (= B II 18), plus a representative sampling of other cases in which the same argument was used. The speech composed for a Syracusan woman in connection with a dispute involving property attributed to Corax's pupil Tisias (Pausanias 6.17.18 = B II 2) may also have been, if the notice is correct, a part of this collection; for neither Corax or Tisias is elsewhere mentioned as being a professional writer of speeches for delivery by others. It is worth noting that the only two names in the late lists of speech parts attributed to Corax with a fifth-century ring to them (*katastasis* and *agōn*) would have been natural designations for the two types of material that any book of model pieces based on *eikos* could be expected to contain: actual specimen arguments, or paired arguments, on a given topic (*agōn*), and the "set-up" (*katastasis*) for each argument—the situational background (however presented) in which the *agōn* was imagined as occurring (compare the two- or three-line summaries that regularly introduce each of the model speeches or pairs of speeches in later collections of *declamationes*).[14]

Further Aristotelian testimony suggests that what applies to Corax applies to two other early writers as well. The *techné* of Callippus and Pamphilus consisted wholly (*Rhet.* 2.23 1400a3–4) of arguments based on a listing and classifying of the usual aims (advantage to oneself, harming one's enemies, benefiting one's friends, and the like) that determine men's actions, particularly criminal ones—the so-called motivational indices (*telika kephalaia*) of later theory (Volkmann 300 ff.). Once again, the topic is irrelevant to any but the proof section of a speech; and—also like *eikos* in this respect—it is restricted enough in its character that it is unlikely to have been able to account for an entire *techné*, unless what was involved was a simple series of examples.

What was true for Tisias and Corax in the mid-fifth century may have been less true for their successors in the next two generations, for Aristotle says explicitly (*Soph. El.* 33 183b29–84b3) that the rhetorical instruction of his own day, unlike that given in dialectic, had progressed well beyond the stage represented by Gorgias, with his model pieces written down and distributed among students to memorize. What Aristotle does not tell us, however, is how far or in what direction progress had gone. What is known about the successors of Tisias and Corax suggests that they continued to deal in illustration rather than analysis, merely replacing sample instances of a single type of speech with a more diversified collection of reusable "speech components." Thrasymachus, for example, produced a series of "Plaints" (*Eleoi*), "piteous in lamentation on the subject of old age and poverty" (Plato, *Phaedr.* 267c7–8). These were obviously models of appeals to emotion which could be injected at appropriate moments into an oration, and they may have been accompanied, as Plato suggests in the same passage, by other pieces designed to stir up (or allay) anger or unpopularity. A long fragment (B IX 10 = 85 B 1) containing the sort of appeal for an end to political factionalism for which there would have been abundant need during the closing years of the Peloponnesian War may be just such a demonstration of how to allay anger.[15] The title "Large [*Megalē*] *Technē*" (B IX 2 = 85 B 3) assigned to a lost work of Thrasymachus would be an appropriate designation for a large collection of such pieces.

Theodorus, usually listed as the first or second of the successors of Tisias and Corax, moved along a somewhat different path, addressing himself to the isolation of speech components with such enthusiasm that he recognized "preparatory" and "supplementary" narrative and proof alongside the normal varieties, as well as refutation, preparatory refutation and supplementary refutation (Plato, *Phaedr.* 266d; Arist., *Rhet.* 3.13 1414b13–15). In similar fashion Evenus of Paros offered "indirect compliments" and "indirect vituperations, in verse for greater ease of memorization" (*Phaedr.* 267a3–50); Licymnius (Arist., *Rhet.* 3.13 1414b16–18) argumentational "byways" (*apoplanēseis*) and "minor branches" (*ozoi*); and Gorgias's pupil Polus entire "choirs of speeches . . . and words . . . to beautify one's eloquence" (*mouseia logōn . . . onomatōn te . . . pros poiēsin euepeias: Phaedr.* 267b10–c3), the latter either borrowed from, or presented as a gift to, his colleague Licymnius.[16]

It is probable that Evenus was offering examples, not analyses, and the same doubtless applies to the items attested for Theodorus, Polus, and Licymnius. The very multitude and diversity of discrete elements implied by the reference to "choirs of speeches" makes the inclusion of description and analysis very unlikely. And the same applies to the "words for beautification" borrowed from—or given to—Licymnius. They could easily have been set forth in the form of two simple lists, depending on whether beauty lay in the sound or the sense (cf. Arist., *Rhet.* 3.2 1405b6–7).[17]

Illustration by example must also have been the favored way of treating the one other speech component that would have played a prominent role in a typical *technē* during this period, the proem. Antiphon (B X 13–14), Critias (88 B 43), and Thrasymachus

(B IX 9) are all said to have composed such pieces; and the openings of Attic orations in the late fifth and early fourth centuries, as well as the transitional passages from the introduction to the body of the speech, often exhibit so stereotyped a pattern that it is reasonable to seek a partial explanation in the availability and influence of written models. By the same token, the absence of any standard method of arranging material once the speaker has launched into the actual presentation of his case in such orations is strong support for the argument that the prescriptive order first attested in Theodectes (mentioned earlier) was *not* part of earlier *techne*. Standardization affects only the content of the recurring commonplaces on law, government, justice, legal procedure, human emotions and desires, and so on, and, to a lesser degree, certain patterns of argumentation. The natural inference is that it was individual elements such as these, not any order in which they were presented or related to each other, that impressed itself on the prospective speaker when he had occasion to consult a *techne*.[18]

What Plato and Aristotle regard as a besetting fault in this phase of protorhetoric—its concern with subdivision into ever minuter and more subtly distinguished categories—need not have been so in a method that was still confined to presenting and identifying examples. Seen in this context, proliferation of classifications and subdivisions is a kind of logical and rhetorical atomism: part of an effort to discover, identify, and illustrate the minimal components of discourse. Mastery of these would be what provided the greatest flexibility and variety when it came to generating actual speeches through a process of recombination. It is only in the context of a systematic study of the psychological bases and ultimate purposes of persuasion that such a method runs the risk of diverting attention from more crucial matters toward an accumulation of trivialities.

It should be stressed, however, that the classifying and naming stage in the development of fifth-century *techne*, even if present in the works of Theodorus and Polus, probably represents an innovation in a tradition that had begun with something much simpler. It was not even characteristic of the work of Theodorus at the beginning of his career, for Aristotle says of a particular variety of *eikos* argument (*Rhet.* 2.24 1400b15–16) that it "constituted the whole of the earlier *technē* of Theodorus." The language recalls that used in reference to Corax (noted earlier) and the natural inference is that, if Theodorus at a certain point was still writing in the manner of Corax, it was because no other method was yet known.[19]

It would have been natural for a collection of sample speech components to be introduced by some sort of preface. There is even reason to believe that a recurring topic in such prefaces was a statement of the writer's claims to teach a true art and a defense of these claims against detractors—a kind of expansion on the oral proclamation or self-advertisement (*epangelma*) that is attributed by Plato to Protagoras (*Prot.* 318e–19a). A stereotyped opening formula from such proems may appear in the phrase "Whoever wishes to learn . . . , let him . . ." which introduces two late-fifth or early fourth-century reference and consultation texts, the medical treatise *Airs, Waters, and Places* and the discussion of the qualities of the ideal statesman known as the Anonymus Iamblichi.[20] Neither work is, strictly speaking, a *technē,* but the distant, mischievous echo in Ovid's *Art of Love* (1.1–2 [tr. Dryden]) may give an idea of the original *technē* context:

> In Cupid's school whoe'er wou'd take Degree [*artem non novit amandi*]
> Must learn his Rudiments, by reading me.

The same sort of context may be the source of the statement attributed, probably accurately, to Gorgias's student Polus (B XIV 3–6), favorably contrasting the control that arises from *technē* and experience (*empeiria*) with the chance (*tychē*) that prevails when men must act without experience to guide them.

Other fifth- and fourth-century texts even suggest a possible reconstruction of two of the objections raised to *technē*'s claims and two of the answers offered.[21] If medicine (or rhetoric, or sophistic, or art X) is truly an art, why is it that (1) so many doctors' patients (rhetoricians' clients, sophists' pupils) die (lose their cases, fail to learn the skills the sophist is paid to teach them); and why is it that (2) so many people have been able and continue to be able to recover from illnesses (become good speakers, learn the skills the sophist teaches) without any medical treatment at all (in times and places where rhetoricians and sophists have never even been heard of)? Both questions are raised in the *Twofold Arguments* (80 B 6.5–6) and in Isocrates 13.14, whereas different versions of the same answers to both questions are to be found in Aristotle, in the Hippocratic treatise *On Ancient Medicine* (3–4), in the speech attributed to the Sophist Protagoras in Plato's dialogue (*Prot.* 327a–b5), and in the praise of the fallen members of the expedition against Thebes in Euripides' *Suppliants.* In reply to (2) it is argued that art capitalizes upon and perfects abilities that exist in rudimentary form in most people and are sufficient in many instances to achieve the same results as art, though less systematically and less predictably. The physician's art rests on a scientific study of proper diet, which is simply the layman's ability to distinguish the food that agrees with him when he is healthy from the food that does not, refined into an ability to distinguish the special foods required by the sick from those required by the healthy. The political skills Protagoras teaches are simply a more sophisticated version of the rough and ready system of respect for others and redress of grievances in which everyone participates and which is an essential prerequisite for any kind of social existence. Similarly, acquiring virtue (*Suppliants* 913–15) is like learning Greek: one does not need a teacher if one grows up amid native speakers (cf. *Twofold Arguments* 6.11), though this does not mean that expert instruction is impossible or that seeking to obtain it is unprofitable. Aristotle presents the rhetorical counterpart to these arguments when at the outset of his treatise he cites the general human ability, whether out of nature or habit, to use speech with a certain degree of effectiveness to support his contention that the whole process can be studied and made more efficient by *techne* (*Rhet.* 1.1 1354a1–11).

Aristotle's definition of rhetoric (see chapter 1) as the art of seeing what is possible in the realm of the persuasive may be similarly influenced by earlier efforts to explain, in answer to question (1), the frequent failure of specialists to do their clients any good. This much is suggested by his own comparison of the rhetorician's failures to those hopeless cases that cannot be made to yield to medical treatment, however expert (*Rhet.* 1.1 1355b12–14). The passage from the *Protagoras* just cited argues in exactly parallel fashion that, given the crucial role of natural ability in the learning process, it is not necessarily a valid criticism of a teacher's claims to point out that some pupils do not respond to instruction (327a4–c4; cf. Isocrates 13.15, and, for what is probably the same contention, *Twofold Arguments* 6.10). *Technē*'s apparent failures may also have been blamed on lack of practice (*meletē, epimeleia*), which a number of fourth-century texts mention alongside natural talent and proper instruction as a prerequisite for the attainment of any sort of expertise.[22]

Suggestions of this sort run the risk, of course, of pressing the evidence too far. The medical answer to (1) may have been analogically extended to rhetoric by Aristotle himself; and (2) is not linked to a *technē* context by any explicit testimony. Even at their most elaborate, however, the reconstructions do not point to the existence of explicit analysis and precepts anywhere except in the proem of a *technē*. Delivery and memory are two standard parts of the later rhetorical treatise which could not have been discussed except through analysis and precepts; but they are, significantly, almost completely ignored by early writers. Only Thrasymachus treated the latter—either briefly (Arist. *Rhet.* 3.1 1403b21–22, 35–36; 1404a13–15 = B IX 11), or just long enough to dismiss it as being a matter of *natura* rather than *ars* (Quintilian 3.3.4 = B IX 19). Memory, aside from a few lines in the *Twofold Arguments* (9.1–6), is not certainly attested as a topic until the Hellenistic period.[23]

What followed the proem in a *technē* must have resembled a collection of rhetorical commonplaces or *topoi*, and the physical layout of such collections may well be the origin of the use of the word *topos* itself (literally, "place," "region"). Students would have been constantly unrolling the papyrus on which a *technē* was written to the spot containing a given model piece—hence, by a natural metonymy, the substitution of the name of the container for that of the contained (cf. French *les plus belles pages* or Italian *pagine scelte* in reference to a collection of extracts). The same semantic evolution would account for the use of the word to designate, not only reusable rhetorical themes or commonplaces, but basic logical techniques (for example, the argument *a fortiori*, known in antiquity as the "*topos* drawn from greater and less").

Zeno of Elea is mentioned by Aristotle as having composed dialectical practice and demonstration texts exactly like the rhetorical ones produced by Gorgias, and it was probably in this form that his celebrated paradoxes first gained currency.[24] Plato may well have the original use of the word in mind when he has Socrates speak of Phaedrus's well-thumbed copy of the *techne* of Tisias as a "well-trodden" one (τόν γε Τεισίαν αὐτὸν πεπάτηκας ἀκριβῶς: *Phaedr.* 273a6). One thumbs one's way through the pages of a book or codex, but one treads one's way through the regions or *topoi* of a papyrus roll. The difficulties later philosophers and rhetorical theorists had in defining the notion of *topos* were probably congenital ones—a result of the fact that in its origin, and for some time thereafter, the word could designate anything habitually located at a given point in a papyrus roll.[25]

Other pieces of standard terminology may also go back to the same protorhetorical, preanalytic stage in the history of the art. Epideictic oratory will then be, in origin, what *epideixis* is in Xenophon's account of Prodicus: not the showing off of one's talent, but the displaying or revealing (orally) of what was already in existence beforehand—in the form of a prememorized piece or all or part of a precomposed written *techne*. And its ultimate use as a designation for ceremonial rather than judicial or political oratory will be a natural result of the fact that ceremonial occasions were the only ones at which recitation of a written (or prememorized) text would have been considered acceptable by a fifth-century audience. The likely reaction to such oral publication in a political or judicial context may be gauged from Thucydides 3.42.3 and 38.2 (those who reopened the debate on Mitylene are men "induced by bribes to work up [*ekponein*] a fancy speech" and "bribed accusers coming up with an *epideixis*") or Aristophanes *Eq.* 345–46 (it is absurd to fancy oneself a clever speaker for "having exhibited [*epideiknys*]" the results of one's "nights of holding forth and chattering to oneself in the streets").[26]

The "unartful persuaders" (*atechnoi pisteis*: witness depositions, oaths, citation of laws, reports of evidence obtained from torture) which are traditionally contrasted with the "artful" persuaders based on argumentation and inference (Arist., *Rhet.* 1.15) may be in origin "extratextual" persuaders—material necessarily presented during the course of a trial by someone other than the pleader himself and hence excluded from the text or texts that served as the ultimate model for what the pleader was to say. The reason for their absence from early *technē* is the same as that for their absence from the later "performance" texts, memorized for delivery on a particular occasion, which became the basis for the published editions of an orator's works. It need have nothing to do with their being, as is usually assumed, unamenable to treatment by the rules of art, or part of the "givens" of a case rather than what the speaker's art enables him to find for himself. There obviously *do* exist rules as to where and when "unartful" persuaders should be employed: how witnesses should be cross-examined, how the validity or relevance of one type of persuader can be upgraded or downgraded to suit the speaker's purpose, etc. Analytical rhetorical treatises, beginning with Aristotle and Anaximenes, have a fair amount to say on such subjects. On the other hand, the givens of a case—if that is what is involved—ought to include not simply witness depositions and the like but the basic facts as set forth in the speaker's narrative—a speech component which, however, always figured among "artful" rather than "unartful" means of persuasion.

Finally, even the term *technē* itself, when used as the object of the verb "write" or coupled with an author's name, is more naturally applied to a practice and demonstration text than it is to a treatise. Anything composed, not to meet the needs of a particular occasion or to make a permanent contribution to the literature of a certain subject, but to exhibit the author's verbal skill in such a way that others could imitate it would become, if written down, a kind of crystallization and memento of that skill. And if an author chose to publish a single such memento, on sale to those who could not attend the actual demonstrations of the skill or who wanted a better record than memory or such notes as they might have taken could provide, it would be natural to think of the document as the "art" of Tisias, or Theodorus, or whoever, captured in writing and so made permanently accessible. Musicological terminology probably provides the closest English parallels, in titles such as the "Art of the Fugue," or the "Art of ———" when applied to a representative selection from the recorded work of a famous singer or instrumentalist.

On the other hand, to speak of "writing an art" or "writing a technique" (*graphein technēn*) when what is meant is writing *about* verbal art or technique may well have been just as strange an expression in fifth-century Greek as it is in modern English. The metonymy only works when the method of presentation is dramatic, narrative, or—to use the fourth-century term—generally "mimetic" in character. Thus one can write the life (*bios*) of a famous man, or the foundation (*ktisis*) or capture (*halōsis*) of a famous city, or the war (*polemos*: cf. Thucydides 1.1) between the Athenians and Peloponnesians. Here the transfer of meaning simply parallels the mapping of a series of events into a verbal medium that is taking place. (Cf., also, the use of *poiein* with a direct object in reference to the "making" or recounting of an episode in verse.) A similar transfer from spoken to written word occurs when the deploying of a speaker's technique is recorded or transmitted in the form of selected samples. Something rather different and more complex is involved when one is recording, not the art itself, but the concepts and principles on which it is based. The latter usage—writing a *technē* in the sense of composing a treatise about the art of verbal composition—eventually becomes quite normal; but it is worth noting that it is not to be found in the work in which the notion of a systematic study of the principles of the art of speaking is first attested. When Plato wishes to refer to the artful composition and delivery of a speech, or to discussions devoted to such subjects, he speaks of proceeding "by means of art" (*technēi*). The phrase *technēn graphein* does appear in his text (*Phaedr.* 261b6–7, 269c6–8, 261c1–2, 275c5 [*technēn . . . en grammasi katalipein*]) but always in reference to the early compositions whose credentials he is rejecting.

The syntactical distinction is a crucial one. If the typical proto-rhetorical *technē* is itself a text set down in writing rather than a set

91

of rules by means of which other texts are generated, it can be both a good deal more than what later ages would recognize as a rhetorical treatise, and also—almost inevitably—a good deal less as well. It need not regard its task the way rhetoric does, as the essentially subordinate one of tending to the manner as against the matter of presentation. The information and ideas it contains may be just as "exemplary" as the way they are treated, in which case it becomes, like some of the neorhetorics mentioned in chapter 1, a means of organizing and improving, at all levels, a speaker's ability to deal with the subjects he is likely to be discussing.

On the other hand, a pedagogy that proceeds exclusively or primarily by examples lacks the analytical metalanguage characteristic of later rhetoric, and with it the ability, either to formulate general principles governing the use of discourse, or relate them to particular instances. It can only illustrate—not explain or justify—the construction of discourses that are long or short or pathetic or rousing or put together out of reusable components in a given manner. It can neither analyze the process of communication itself nor—as Plato points out (*Phaedr.* 268a8–69c5)—give the student the means of knowing when one sort of speech should be used rather than another. It proceeds, as Aristotle complains, the way a cobbler would if he attempted to transmit his art by giving pupils a ready-made pair of shoes to imitate (*Soph. El.* 33.183b29 ff.), or a set of soles, lasts, laces, and heels. Unlike rhetoric, it fails to present its examples in the context of a theoretical discussion of the anatomy, pathology, and proper functioning of the human foot, and of the ways that knowledge of the first two makes it possible to maximize the third. Sample speech parts, like sample shoe parts, can be constructed in such a way as to minimize idiosyncrasy and so point more clearly than would a random selection of such objects to the general principles on which their construction is based. To this extent they do bring us a stage nearer to true rhetorical analysis than does Euripidean exposition or the prose of the Ionian logographers mentioned in chapter 4, with their attempt to isolate a core of true statements or normal Greek usage within the larger conglomerate of inherited artistic discourse. But a paradigm is still a paradigm, even if it is a generalized one: a confessed wrongdoer (Helen), a man accused of attempted treason (Palamedes), and the glorious dead are Gorgias's ostensible subject matter, not the problem of establishing criminal intent and sufficient motivation, or limiting the applicability of circumstantial evidence, or finding adequate praise for a supreme act of self-sacrifice.

Moreover, there is still no effort to deal with the calculated series of choices that must take place if the general, once formulated, is to be reembodied in a new verbal texture uniquely suited to the speaker's purpose. Such suitability to speaker's purpose was touched upon by Gorgias under the heading of *kairos* (objectively, "seasonableness" or "the proper season"; subjectively, a sense for exactly when the proper season is at hand). But his remarks on the subject were, according to the one surviving reference to them, "of no value" (Dionysius of Halicarnassus, *De comp. verb.* 12 p. 45.12– 15 Usener-Radermacher). Probably this aspect of eloquence was left largely, just as Plato complains (*Phaedr.* 268a8–69c5), to the ingenuity of the student. It is even possible that Gorgias "discussed" the principle in the same way Pindar discussed it—via brief pronouncements as to its necessity or desirability, inserted into passages that illustrate in one way or another how it operates (cf. *Olympian* 13.48; *Pythian* 1.81, 4.286, 9.78; *Nemean* 1.18).

That late fifth-century *techne* availed itself of the wider possibilities just indicated can be extensively documented (see chapter 6); and the consequences of this fact for one's understanding of the history of rhetoric will be fairly easy to show. It is harder to assess the full significance of the limitations of this *techne*. The analytical metalanguage characteristic of fourth-century treatises may have had purely oral antecedents of which all reports have disappeared. Yet the completeness of the disappearance—if that is what is involved—suggests otherwise; as does the relative slowness with which, during the course of the following century, explicit rhetorical theory or works that give evidence of having been composed in accordance with theory begin to appear. The process, as will be seen (chapter 7), is prolonged enough to suggest that advances in or toward theory were committed to writing piecemeal, as soon as they were made. And the process begins late enough to suggest that such advances were inextricably linked to the development of new forms of written communication, hence inconceivable in the predominantly oral cultural context in which the model written discourse of the late fifth century had first arisen.

Six

The Range and Limits of *Techne*

The discourse components illustrated for use by prospective speakers in fifth-century *techne* are usually assumed—on the basis of explicit statements by Aristotle (*Rhet.* 1.1 1354b22–27) and Isocrates (*Against the Sophists* 19)—to belong largely or exclusively to the realm of courtroom eloquence.[1] It is also assumed—on the basis of what is implied by Aristotle and Plato (*Rhet.* 1.1 1354b16–21, 3.13 1414a31–b18; *Phaedr.* 266d1–69c5)—that they were, as a rule, narrowly stylistic in character (rhetorical doublets, varying means of compressing or expanding an argument, fancy words for ordinary objects, etc.) and directed toward influencing audience attitudes (recipes for appealing to pity, rousing indignation, and the like). Enough specimens of *techne* have already been cited, however, to make all three of these generalizations questionable: it is hard to see, for example, how they apply to Prodicus's Choice of Heracles, or Gorgias's Funeral Oration, or the Paradoxes of Zeno of Elea. And further study of the genre tends to strengthen these initial doubts.

The single most frequent way of referring to the "components" in which *techne* dealt is by abstract nouns ending in *-logia,* and even a partial list of those attested for the period is sufficient to indicate that the essential thing they had in common was their "reusability," not their "instrumentality" in the process of framing a message for better transmission. An idea, a principle, or even a set of facts that an author could be expected to have frequent occasion to use would be quite as likely to find its place in the list as a turn of style or a trick of argument. Thus one finds—alongside *eleeinologia* (appeal to pity), *gnōmologia* (use of maxims), *eikonologia* (use of comparisons or examples), *diplasiologia* (doublets), and *palillogia* (summary)—rubrics of a different kind such as *dikaiologia* (arguing the rights and wrongs of a case), and *brachylogia* and *makrologia*. (The last two terms probably refer to the discussion of subjects requiring, respectively, brief presentation and extended presentation—the short questions and answers of the eristics as against the long, continuous expositions of the Sophists, for example [cf. Plato, *Prot.* 334c–35c],[2] or the series of culminating moments recommended by Pindar [for example, *Pythian* 9.77–78] for narrative and panegyric as against the exhaustive cataloguing favored by epic.)

Later reports are in the habit of interpreting such terms in a narrowly rhetorical sense wherever possible—brachylogy and macrology, for example, as the art of inflating small matters and downplaying large ones by making length of treatment seem a valid index of the importance of the subject treated. There is rarely any need to do so, however, and it often makes more sense to assume that the techniques referred to were devised for essentially "nonrhetorical" purposes. The appeal to probability (*eikos, eikotologia*), for example, is for Plato tantamount to preferring appearance over truth (*Phaedr.* 267a6–7); and in citing examples of it both he and Aristotle emphasize less the basic principle involved than the devious uses to which it can be put. When, for whatever reason, a defendant needs to impugn a given reconstruction of events, the appeal to *eikos* will allege that the very likelihood of the reconstruction tells against its correctness: no one would have been likely to commit a crime for which he was destined to be the most likely suspect (Plato, *Phaedr.* 267d7–e5; Arist., *Rhet.* 2.23 1400a7–17). In this fashion the argument from *eikos* becomes purely rhetorical in character: an alternative to straightforward presentation of facts or alleged facts. It is a speculative digression into what might have been expected to happen in a given situation, and a digression presented in such a way as to take the attention away from those facts that do not support the speaker's contention as to what *did* happen. Alternatively, it may even be nothing more than an effort to win acceptance for a view because of the novelty and ingenuity with which it is formulated and defended.

The situation is quite different when Aristotle has occasion to mention *eikos* outside the context of a discussion of early *technē*. There he is able to see *eikos* as a perfectly acceptable part of the dialectical component of rhetoric: the use of statements that are generally but not universally true (*Rhet.* 1.2 1357a32–b1; 2.25 1402b12–16). It is hard to believe that he was the first to conceive the matter in this fashion, or that *eikos* had always been invoked, as Plato suggests, in conscious preference to truth. Often it must have recommended itself as the only means of reaching a decision in the face of conflicting or inadequate testimony about past events or the absence of certain prognosis about the future. And on such occasions it would have taken its place alongside testimony, oaths, and various types of inference as an indispensable tool of inquiry: as much a part of criminology and jurisprudence—or historical and scientific speculation—as of rhetoric narrowly conceived.

The same could be said of the *telika kephalaia*, illustrated by Callippus and Pamphilus, or of *dikaiologia*, which is simply the *status definitivus* of later theory and so, along with the *status qualitativus* of Gorgias's *Helen* and the *status coniecturalis* of his *Palamedes* (see chapter 5) an anticipation of the three basic categories familiar from Hellenistic and post-Hellenistic theory. The term *status* (= Greek *stasis*) is first attested in Isocrates' pupil Naucrates (B XXXI 3), but it is clear from the way Aristotle and his contemporary Anaximenes refer to the distinctions on which *status* theory was based (Kennedy 306) that something similar must have already existed as an established part of *technē* in their day and perhaps even earlier. Each of the model sets of speeches that comprise the tetralogies of Antiphon illustrate a different one of the three *status* recognized by later theoreticians, and this may well be the result of a conscious effort at completeness on the part of the author or compiler.

The earliest name for what was produced by combining a suitable number of these "-ologies" seems to have been *logōn* (not *rhetorikē*) *technē*, a technique of "words" or "discourse" rather than of rhetoric.[3] Like the corresponding Isocratean expressions that refer to knowledge (*epistēmē*) practice (*meleteia, epimeleia*), or education (*paideia*) in *logoi*, the phrase *logōn technē* can also designate the oral art of which the written *technē* is a record; and it has the wide range of meaning one would expect, given the fact that *logos* can refer to "reason" or "reasoning" as well as "speech," and to the rational structure in things or subjects as much as to the reasoning that reveals it. One late fifth-century text mentions mastery of this technique as a possible means of securing general recognition for one's merits, and these merits include wisdom, bravery, and general excellence (*aretē*) whether in its entirety or any one of its parts (Anonymus Iamblichi 1.1 and 2.7). The range of talents is far too wide to be revealed to the world in courtroom performances, however brilliant. In Xenophon's *Memorabilia* (1.1.31–37) *logōn technē* is what Critias, acting on behalf of the Thirty, forbids Socrates to teach. More precisely, as Critias explains in reply to Socrates' disingenuous inquiries as to what the expression means, it is talk about "shoemakers and carpenters and blacksmiths"—a fairly clear synecdoche for the Socratic elenchus and the philosophical inquiry with which it was intimately linked (cf. Plato, *Gorgias* 490e, *Symp.* 221e4–7).

In the *Twofold Arguments* (5.3–4) mastery of *logōn technē* is regarded as inseparable from a capacity for informed discourse on all possible subjects. Elsewhere it may have been defined more narrowly, but the notion was doubtless broad enough to include both the art of long speeches that belongs to the Sophist or rhetor and the art of brief question and answer that belongs to the dialectician. Plato represents both Gorgias and the Sophist Protagoras as laying claim to expertise in both (*Gorgias* 449b9–c3, *Prot.* 328e4–29b5); and the term *rhetoric,* if it is not in fact a Platonic invention, may have been originally contrasted with dialectic as one of two major subdivisions within the larger category of *logōn technē*. But the distinction, first attested in the *Gorgias,* by which dialectic comes to be regarded as the sole means for the discovery and articulation of truth and rhetoric simply a producer of persuasion, is almost certainly a Platonic innovation, designed to downgrade the achievements of all the "nondialectical"—i.e., non-Eleatic—masters of *logos* who preceded Socrates. The earliest non-Platonic hint of such a distinction is Isocrates' contrast (3.8) between "men of speech" (*rhētorikous*) who are able to persuade the multitude, and "men of counsel" (*eubouloi*) who do the same thing when they converse (*dialechthōsi*) among themselves. And the passage, written in the 370s, appears in the course of a defense of the art of speaking that may well be a reply to the *Gorgias.*

The inclusiveness of *logōn technē,* whether in its "dialectical" or "rhetorical" manifestation, is further attested to by surviving fragments and titles, over and above those mentioned in the preceding chapter. All the published work of Protagoras fits the *logōn technē* category—if, as is often assumed, the various titles cited for him are simply variant ways of referring to the separate items—political, logical, anthropological, epistemological—in his "Knock-down Arguments" (*Kataballontes Logoi:* 80 B 1) or "Reasonings Pro and Con" (*Antilogiai:* 80 B 5). The antithetical arrangement of this collection may have been the model for that of the *Twofold Arguments,* which recalls Plato's *Protagoras* both in its enumeration of examples to show that good is relative (cf. 334a–c) and in its discussion of the teachability or nonteachability of excellence (*aretē*). Mathematics and wrestling seem to have been among the activities whose claims to being teachable arts were knocked down (cf. 80 B 7–8)—perhaps as a foil to Protagoras's defense of his own discipline, perhaps in order to be reestablished once it was time for the Argument-Con to be succeeded by the Argument-Pro.

Gorgias's famous treatise *On Not Being* is less obviously a *technē* than the *Helen* and the *Palamedes;* but it resembles them closely in that it is a collection of incompatible arguments. Each of the first two in a series of three positions is abandoned as soon as the defense of the position is finished, whereupon Gorgias passes immediately to a new position which concedes the point that was just being argued. This suggests that here too the aim is to provide a set of tools that will be useful in facing as wide a variety of opponents and debating situations as possible. If the initial argument maintaining that nothing exists is inappropriate or unsuccessful, the debater can always proceed to the less extreme positions that follow: first that, even supposing something does exist, it is unknowable; and then that knowledge, even supposing it is possible, is not necessarily communicable.

The semantic distinctions between apparent synonyms for which the Sophist Prodicus was famous were probably offered as examples of how to facilitate debate by removing ambiguities and misunderstandings. The encomia of Heracles and agriculture which he is known or inferred to have written belong to the same genre as the defense of Helen produced by Gorgias: *singularum rerum laudes* (see chapter 5).[4]

Finally, in the long papyrus fragments usually thought to come from the work *On Truth* written by an Antiphon who may or may not be identical with the orator, both the radicalism of the critique of the social and judicial process offered and its pared-down, almost mathematically precise style suggests the presence of an effort, partially for the purposes of demonstration, to push a highly individualistic moral calculus to the extreme formulation of which it was capable. If the work *On Concord*, of which only brief fragments survive (87 B 45–48, 52, 55, 65, 67–71) is by the same Antiphon, it may have been a companion piece, devoted to insisting on the advantages of social consensus in equally extreme and uncompromising fashion. A third Antiphontic piece, concerned with "dispelling grief" (*alypia*) is explicitly referred to as a *technē* (87 A 6), and this is much more likely to have been a sample *consolatio* or series of *consolationes* than a treatise on psychotherapy. It may be the source of three fragments (87 B 49–51) on the brevity and misery of life and the disappointments of marriage. Their content, at any rate, suggests what was to become a standard consolatory *topos:* the addressee's particular, individual grief is minimized by emphasizing the transient, unsatisfactory character of all the things men seek after and value most highly.[5]

The polymath Hippias, with his varied investigations into history, geography, chronology, etymology, and mathematics, is the only major Sophist who may have been extensively involved, like his Ionian contemporaries (discussed in chapter 5), in the production of reference and consultation texts. But though the *technē* format could hardly have done justice to his encyclopedic attainments, it need not follow that he was a voluminous writer. He may well have preferred oral publication, which would certainly have been a more convincing tribute to the powers of memory for which he was famous (cf. A11). It is worth noting that the only one of his written works of whose format we are certain is the so-called *Trōikos Logos*—an exemplary protrepsis in which Nestor instructs the young Neoptolemus in "many legitimate and noble pursuits" that will win him glory (Plato, *Hipp. mai.* 286a7–b4).

The musicologist Damon's analysis of the "ethical" effect of musical modes might also seem ill suited to presentation as a *technē*, but if identical with the piece referred to by Philodemus (*De mus.* 4.33.37 = 37 B 2) it took the form of a speech before the Areopagus. The speech was presumably a fictitious one, whether attributed to Damon himself or some historical or mythological character contemporary with the period of that body's supposed preeminence in Athenian public life (compare the brief digression on the blend of constraint and liberty necessary for good government delivered before the Areopagus by Athena at Aesch., *Eumenides* 696–704).

Presentation of an argument in the form of an imaginary speech is certainly not a sure sign that the work involved is a *technē*, but we know that *technai* were in fact composed in the form on occasion, and it fits very well with the *technē* writer's purpose.[6] It allows the argument to come from the mouth of the person most qualified to present it (Nestor, for example) or to be addressed to the audience (the Areopagus) most capable of appreciating and judging it. There could hardly be a more effective way of underlining the paradigmatic value of what is being said.

The device also minimizes the difference between the format of a didactic work and the format a speaker will use when he recapitulates its teachings for the benefit of others. This may well explain why it is so difficult to find a piece of fifth-century Attic prose standing completely outside the *technē* tradition. The very decision to write in Attic could have been in many cases the result of a desire to use the dialect in which the contents of a *technē* would be reproduced or its sample procedures imitated. Thus Gorgias writes in Attic, though he was born in an Ionian colony and grew up in the Doric cultural world of eastern Sicily. Had he been producing a consultation or performance text, intended for simple comprehension rather than imitation by Athenian readers or hearers, he might have been expected, like Herodotus, or the earliest Atthidographer (Hellanicus), or the earliest Attic logographer (Pherecydes), to take the easier, more precedented course of writing in Ionic. Similar considerations will explain why one other piece of non-Ionic prose attested for this period is also a *technē*: the Doric *Twofold Arguments* (presumably composed for the use of aspiring speakers in the Peloponnese or Magna Graecia).[7]

Even specific commentary on contemporary events tends, when offered as a written text, to appear in the guise of a *technē*. The pseudo-Xenophontic *Constitution of Athens* is such a commentary, and there is good reason to accept the view of those who regard it as some sort of exercise or *paignion*.[8] The author professes strong oligarchic, hence anti-Periclean, feelings. Yet he makes use of what is, to judge from the Thucydidean contexts in which parallels to it appear, a pro-Periclean, democratic view of the crucial importance of Athenian sea power. The influence of the lower classes in Athenian life is seen as an inevitable consequence of their role in manning the fleet, and the resulting political system as a morally reprehensible, but completely consistent and effective arrangement, to which there is no viable alternative. This peculiar combination of positions makes it hard to identify the author's exact political background and sympathies, and it is equally hard to be sure of the date of the piece itself, or its general tone, or the circumstances of its composition, or its immediate purpose:

> It has been argued from various references and significant silences that it was written before 431, before 430 but after 431, before 425, after 425, before the production of the *Knights* and after it. Some have seen it as the work of an older man who would curb the youthful hotheads

among the oligarchs, others as that of an extremist contemptuous of academic reformers and moderates, ready to surrender not only the empire but his city's independence if only the hated democracy can be got rid of; some find in it a gay irony, others *bitterer Ernst*; . . . it is addressed to Athenians, to Spartans, to the discontented oligarchs of the empire.[9]

Since this was published (1940), dates as early as the late 440s have been suggested,[10] and the author seen—from an American perspective of the late 1960s—as a recent adherent to the Athenian "new right": dedicated to the oligarchic cause with a convert's zeal, but unable at times to suppress completely the memories of the enthusiasm with which, in his democratic days, the vision of world hegemony through sea power had inspired him.[11] All such problems disappear or become irrelevant if the author is simply making a compendium of arguments—good, bad, and indifferent—for the attributing to Athens of certain virtues—formidable might in international affairs and the internal stability to back it up—which even an enemy would have to admire. It is an easy thing, as Socrates points out apropos of the model funeral oration delivered by him in the *Menexenus* (236b3–6), to praise Athens before an audience of Athenians. The hard thing, presumably—and we have the authority of Isocrates (*Helen* 8–9) for the premium his predecessors put on hard cases as a means of training a prospective speaker— would be to praise the Athenians before Spartans or any other hostile audience. And this is probably what pseudo-Xenophon is attempting, whether his work is a master's demonstration of how such a thing should be done, or a pupil's effort to imitate his master's performance or work out an idea suggested by him.

It would doubtless have been possible to find many of the arguments the author uses in totally committed, serious, and (as a consequence) oral statements of opinion by oligarchs; but there is nothing to indicate the actual political position (if he had one) of the author himself. In view of the extreme silliness of some of his pro-oligarchic contentions—especially those posited on the assumption that Athens is a topsy-turvy but completely viable world to itself where the good is, by definition, anything that benefits bad men—one cannot even exclude the possibility that he was a radical democrat. Whatever his politics, he would doubtless have been pleased to see how successful the scholarship of later generations has been in making his arguments work for a wide variety of occasions and speakers. Few *technai* can have achieved their basic purpose so well.

The most memorable occasion for the use of such a *technē* was probably the debate reported, or invented, by Thucydides (1.67 ff.), during the course of which Corinthian envoys glorify Athenian energy and resourcefulness in an effort to goad a Spartan audience into taking action against the state that is challenging their position as leaders of Greece. The speech of the Corinthians is usually seen as a particularly brilliant Thucydidean stroke—"ein Lob das um so schwerer wiegt weil es aus des Gegners Munde kommt."[12] But here as elsewhere Thucydides must share the credit with the earlier masters of the intellectual and pedagogical tradition to which he belongs. Taken as a whole, his history provides the best available means for estimating the full range and possibilities of fifth-century *technē*. The speeches attributed to leading statesmen and generals at critical points in the course of the Peloponnesian War constitute a huge chrestomathy of political and military eloquence, obviously drawing on the work of predecessors and contemporaries, but dwarfing in bulk and significance every other *technē* of which we have any record.

These speeches were composed, according to the author's own account (1.22.1), "in the way it seemed to me that each of the speakers would have said what was most called for (*ta deonta*) concerning the matter at hand, sticking as closely as possible to the general sense (*xympasa gnōmē*) of what was actually said." Most Thucydideans, rightly I believe, have concluded from this passage that "historical" accuracy is a secondary consideration in the portion of the history devoted to *logoi*. It is adhered to "as closely as possible," but only to the extent that what was in fact said was compatible with what should have been said (*ta deonta*). Contrast the passage immediately following (1.22.2–3), on the great pains taken by the writer in gathering and comparing eyewitness accounts of the events he is to relate. There "the way it seemed to me that things would have *happened*" is just as emphatically rejected as a criterion for reporting *events* as, in the preceding sentence, "the way it seemed to me things would have been *said*" was accepted as a criterion in reporting *logoi*.[13] Thucydides is committed to making the best case possible for the positions actually advanced in the speeches of which he chooses to include an account in his history—to producing, in other words, a series of *logōn technai* as well as *logoi*— and to this end he is willing to retain no more of what was actually said than an approximation to "the general sense." If the gap between this sense and what ought to have been said was too great, consistency would require that he not report a speech at all rather than ask the reader to waste time over what was not worth remembering or imitating.

This severely normative way of reporting speeches as parts of a complex *logōn technē* is the natural counterpart to the intention, expressed at the end of the same chapter (1.22.4), to record, so far as events are concerned, not simply what happened but "what will happen again at some time in much the same or similar fashion, human nature being what it is." Preoccupation with the constant and recurring aspects of events—what will *happen* again and again—is exactly balanced by concentration on what is constant and recurring in discourse: what men will have occasion to *say* again and again "in much the same fashion." Both speeches and narrative thereby become a possession "for always" (*es aiei:* 1.22.4). The phrase is usually translated "for eternity," but it can just as easily mean "for any occasion that may arise." The text of Thucydides is a document available for consultation any time a model for words or a precedent for the course that events seem to be taking is required.

The uniform style of Thucydides' speeches, the obscurity that often results from the complexity and compression of their argumentation, and the frank and at times brutal outspokenness with which they are capable of arguing for a foreign policy based on pure expedience have often been adduced, with good reason, to support the view that, so far from accurate reports of what was actually said on the occasions when they were purportedly delivered, they cannot even resemble anything which *might* have been said.[14] But for "might have been said" one should probably substitute "might have been said before an actual assembly or jury." It is not necessary to maintain that the most characteristic features of Thucydidean thought and style were totally unknown in Athens at the time when most of the speeches are supposed to have been delivered.[15] What was impossible in a publicly spoken *logos* might well have been possible in a written *technē,* or in a private *epideixis* based on it.

The case for the "undeliverability" of the speeches becomes even stronger if one abandons the frequent assumption that the gap between speech as delivered and speech as reported stems from Thucydides' desire to use his speeches primarily as a vehicle for his own analyses of the crucial issues and underlying historical causes at work at the time of delivery.[16] This assumption will explain why Thucydides has a speaker say what he should have said rather than what he did say, but not why, as happens more often than not, two opposite analyses of a situation are given, both of which—if Thucydides is true to the program of 1.22.1—contain what "should" have been said. The presentation of opposite arguments makes sense, however, if Thucydides is simply making the best possible case for a given position, without thereby claiming absolute validity for the argument presented. By virtue of the number of good cases made for positions whose maintenance he regards as mistaken or even foolhardy, he commits himself to conceiving "what was called for" in general rather than particular terms. No speaker fails to make the kind of case that would be, under certain circumstances, the one Thucydides would like to see made and accepted by an audience. All things are fair in their season, and so the writer of a *technē* for all seasons (*es aiei*) must show how all things are fair—or, failing that, how opposite things are fair, letting this polarity stand for the whole spectrum of possibilities.

The general arguments favored by this paradigmatic conception of the function of *logos* in the history sometimes predominate at the expense, or even to the exclusion, of those particular considerations noted by Thucydides as having had a significant effect on the decisions the speeches were intended to influence. Thus Athenian interest in the Corcyrean alliance as a means of acquiring an ally favorably positioned on the route to Sicily is mentioned in 1.44.3 as a major consideration in determining the Athenian decision to take Corcyra's side in her quarrel with Corinth; but it is given the briefest of mentions in the Corcyrean request for Athenian aid, largely devoted as that request is to general arguments in favor of an interventionist policy in foreign affairs. Even more strikingly, the inventory of those financial resources that would, in Pericles' view, enable Athens to survive the purely defensive conduct of the war he favors appears in indirect discourse (2.13.3–6) as part of the contents of a speech made to the Athenians *after* the decision to go to war had already been taken (1.145). There is nothing of this, however, in the general discussion of the strength of Athens' sea-based military power by means of which Pericles is represented as having persuaded the Athenians to make that decision in the first place (1.140–44). The result is an improbable sequence of events (or *logoi*), and one wonders whether Thucydides did not regard the specific details of the economic situation as a kind of "extratextual" persuader (see chapter 5)—to be excluded, like witness depositions and other aspects of a typical court case that would not find their way into a future speaker's model text, from the written *technē* that he assigns to Pericles in the first book.

The demands of *technē* also seem to have been decisive in determining which speeches, out of all those of whose content Thucydides could have had some knowledge, were chosen for inclusion in the history. Intrinsic excellence and influence on the course of events were evidently less essential considerations than the need to create an extensive, representative sampling of those themes most likely to recur in political and military discourse. Thus one has—to use the single most striking example—four speeches dealing with the treatment of defecting allies: two arguing for leniency and two for severity, two from basically utilitarian considerations and two from considerations of justice.

	Justice	Expediency
Severity	the Thebans against the Plataeans (3.60–67)	Cleon against the Mityleneans (3.37–40)
Leniency	the Plataeans in their own defense (3.53–59)	Diodotus for the Mityleneans (3.42–48)

The defense of interventionism in foreign policy has already been noted as the theme of the speech of the Corcyreans, balanced by the opposite case for caution (Corinth). The advantages of war waged by a land confederation of independent states are presented by the Corinthians at the meeting of the Peloponnesian League (1.120–24), as are those of an imperial sea power in the next speech of the book (1.140–44). The case for strategic surrender is balanced against that for resistance to the end in the Melian dialogue; as are the claims which the general good, as embodied in the democratic state, can make on individual loyalties and efforts (Pericles at Athens in Book 2), against the claims of the prominent individual against the democratic state (Alcibiades at Sparta in Book 6); and those of experience in the techniques of battle as the best means to victory (2.87) against those of bravery and resourcefulness (2.86). Hermocrates urges on the Syracusan assembly the need to forget domestic differences in the face of the threat of aggression from a foreign foe (6.33–34), and Athenagoras urges on the same assembly the necessity of not forgetting legitimate party aims in the face of a real or alleged threat from abroad (6.36–40). Athenagoras's speech is, of course, foolish in the extreme at the juncture in which it is delivered; but replace Hermocrates with his son-in-law Dionysius (the future tyrant) and the Athenian threat with a Carthaginian one, change the date from 415 to 405, and it is easy to see how there could have been a place and time for the attack on partisan manipulation of a foreign threat to upset the delicate balance of power between parties and interest groups on which democratic institutions rest. It is possible (see Dover's note to 6.38.3–5), but not necessary, that Thucydides had the events of 405 specifically in mind when he wrote the passage: he did not have to wait for the advent of a Dionysius to become aware of the enduring value (as against the immediate irrelevance and folly) of Athenagoras's argument.

Naturally, matters are rather more complicated than such a schematic survey can suggest. It is often parts of speeches that stand in the relation of model opposites. Arguments for unlimited debate (a precondition for any rational decision) and against unlimited debate (a field day for misapplied ingenuity) make up the balancing opening sections of the speeches of Diodotus and Cleon in Book 3; and the strict versus the loose interpretations of the duty of colony toward mother city is debated within the larger airing of issues between Corinthians and Corcyreans in Book 1. If it is rare to find two speeches maintaining the same position, it is equally rare to find a single argument accounting for a whole speech. Thucydides wants, so far as possible, to provide a record of positions actually taken, and on occasion, perhaps, even to indicate how a position was shaped by an individual speaker.[17] If this can be done without compromising the paradigmatic value of the speech as a whole, nothing in his stated program prevents him from doing so. He may even be deliberately exploring the possibilities opened up by the dual character of the book: a gigantic Attic *logōn technē* concerned with deliberative speech on political and military matters, embedded in an equally ambitious Ionian reference and consultation text on the political and military history of a particular war.

Such refinements do not, however, prevent his work from occupying a central position in the history of protorhetorical *technē,* or from providing us with the best single means of gauging the overall character of a discipline of which much briefer records survive elsewhere. Fifth-century education toward eloquence would—at its best—have stood in approximately the same relation to the systematic treatment of the subject found in Aristotle's *Rhetoric* and later treatises as do the political speeches of Thucydides' history to the sections of Aristotle's *Politics* (basically, Books 4– 6) which deal systematically with the same range of phenomena. Richer, more wide-ranging, more subtle and suggestive than anything found in the *Politics,* this Thucydidean "best" is nevertheless inferior to its Aristotelian counterpart in certain definite ways. For it is as difficult to extract a single coherent set of political and military principles from Thucydides as it is to extract a coherent political platform from pseudo-Xenophon. Thucydides has been alternatively seen as pro-Athenian or pro-Spartan, imperialist or anti-imperialist, militarist or pacifist, determinist or antideterminist in his view of the nature of the historical process. And in the absence of any general statement of position on such questions it is often impossible to be sure why or to what extent he felt the views in a given discourse were applicable to the situations that produced it. One has, at most, certain situations in which events seem to confirm or refute the interpretation of them given by a particular speaker,[18] or instances of the same general argument applied, contrary to the historian's normal practice, to several situations, one of which is more suited to the argument than another. The latter method is crucial to creating the set of parallels often noted between the "Archidamian" and Sicilian books of the history.[19] One of the purposes of these parallels must be to focus the readers' attention on the relationship between *logos* and *ergon,* analysis and actuality. Are the cases of the Athenians and Corinthians for and against imperialism (1.68–78) more or less valid than their restatements by the Athenian Euphemus and the Syracusan Hermocrates at the conference in Camarina reported at 6.76–87, and if so, why? Are Pericles (2.60–64) and Alcibiades (6.18) equally justified in arguing the folly of turning back once an initial decision in favor of a policy of aggressive interventionism in international affairs has been made?

But though such questions are raised at times, Thucydides does not provide definite answers. It is only events themselves, whether those that Thucydides himself presents or those apropos of which similar speeches will be delivered in the future, which can vindicate or refute the way a given speaker has applied his *technē.* And it is only repeated failures in the application of Thucydidean models and repeated successes with different ones which might indicate whether and in what ways Thucydidean *technē* could be itself improved. Like the less ambitious, less extensive *technai* of his contemporaries, it is subject to the same limitations mentioned at the end of chapter 5. Thucydides' text gives little reason to believe that its author possessed either the desire to focus on a speaker's grasp of the particular that is necessary if a persuasive process is to be demonstrated or analyzed in its entirety, or the command of metalanguage that would permit him to discuss the degree to which any set of general principles is illustrated by a particular piece of successful or unsuccessful persuasion. Explicit analyses of oratorical performance are always brief and jejune: Brasidas was "a good speaker for a Spartan" (4.84.2); Pericles knew when to encourage and when to restrain his Athenian audience (2.65.9); words lost their normal meanings in the debates and deliberations of the Peloponnesian War (3.84.4—a single sentence, followed, in the manner of the *technē* writer, by a whole paragraph of examples).

The absence of detailed analysis, not only in Thucydides, but everywhere in protorhetoric, is consistent enough to give strong support to what was suggested at the end of chapter 5, that the metalanguage that would have made analysis possible simply did not exist at the time to any significant degree. (Had it existed, the "changing of the meaning of words" in relation to their referents of which Thucydides complains might have been easier to detect.)

Persuasive speech limited to the needs of a particular situation, on the other hand, obviously did exist, and Thucydides must have been quite familiar with it. It makes at least one brief, incongruous appearance in his own text—in the passage (4.27–28) where Cleon is maneuvered by his opponents in the Athenian assembly into taking command of reinforcements for Sphacteria. Here Thucydides seems to have decided, for whatever reason, to reproduce some of what was actually said (or could have been said) on a public occasion rather than what should have been said.[20] The absence of imitation of this sort from most written prose is partially owing to the fact that, up to a point, *technē* could function just as well or better without it; but at the same time one suspects that this absence was somehow related to the further absence—from all discourse, not simply from written prose—of the rhetorical metalanguage that was to become commonplace during the course of the next century.

If the relationship is a causal one, absence of metalanguage may well be the determining factor: written Attic prose in the fifth century is a calculated, artificial prose and cannot admit the particular except to the degree that it can be explicitly related, through some sort of metalanguage, to the general principles that justify and explain its presence. But it is equally possible that the relationship between cause and effect was just the reverse: analytical metalanguage can only develop on the basis of a close study and comparison of particular pieces of persuasive eloquence, and such close examination is only possible when these pieces of eloquence are available in written form.

If one must choose between these two theories, the second is more likely to be right. The deed is father to the thought, and written eloquence the prerequisite for an analysis of the workings of eloquence in general, just as, in all probability, it was the physical existence of the practice and demonstration text—the tangible, localizable "place" from which a whole series of oral performances emanated—which made it possible for Thucydides to speak in terms of the "general sense" that might be common to a number of different speeches, or for Prodicus to offer both three- and forty-drachma versions of the same *logos*.

In practice, however, the two explanations are complementary rather than contradictory. Whatever the original point or points of departure, the art of rhetorical analysis, on the one hand, and, on the other, the ability to reproduce in writing the unfolding of a particular piece of persuasive communication as fully as the medium will allow, seem to have developed *pari passu*, influencing and influenced by each other at every stage. The origin of rhetoric out of protorhetoric is inseparable from the history of the development of fourth-century Attic prose.

THE FOURTH
CENTURY

Seven

Rhetoric and Prose

Turning down an invitation to hear a drama or public epideixis in favor of an evening at home with a book was doubtless as unusual in early fourth-century Athens as staying at home from an opera or concert in order to read the score would be today—though much more unusual then than it was to become a century or so later. By 300 B.C. educated taste, or the quality of home entertainment, had been radically transformed. Few political or philosophical debates of the early Hellenistic period could hope to be as exciting as those recorded in the dialogues of Plato or the orations of Demosthenes and his contemporaries; and there would be many who shared Aristotle's taste (*Poetics* 6.1450b18–19) for closet drama, or who looked to historiography rather than the stage for moving, semifictionalized evocations of heroic grandeur and catastrophe. A public of hearers had been replaced, to a remarkable extent, by a public of readers and, concurrently, the *technē* of the fifth century by a true reading text. The writers of such texts aspired to as total a recreation as possible of the effect of oral communication, and so to an ability to compete for public attention which *technē* never possessed or sought. The evolution from *technē* to reading text proceeded faster in some areas than in others, but strikingly parallel lines of development can be traced in all three of the major prose genres of the period: philosophical dialogue, oratory, and historiography.

Progress was most rapid in the realm of philosophy. Already by the 380s, demonstrations of dialectical technique such as those written by Zeno and memorized by his students had given way to the Socratic dialogues of Plato and his contemporaries. These were efforts at a full-scale revelation and recreation of Socratic *ēthos* as well as Socratic method, and at a mode of presentation that would give the whole flavor of philosophical debate as experienced by the listening spectator. One could thereby enjoy the contributions of observers and minor participants as well as of questioner and respondent, the play of personalities as well as arguments, and the excitement of argumentative ploys, digressions, false turns, and sudden *peripeteiai* as well as the sequence of demonstrations that led to a conclusion or concluding *aporia*. The reading text that resulted was not simply a record for future use of some of the productive modes of argumentation that can emerge from such debates. It was a substitute for actual attendance at a debate staged between the great masters of dialectic—a means of "showing to the play-loving Athenians pedagogically serious eristic in action."[1]

In oratory, whether because of tradition or psychological inhibitions or simple inertia, progress was slower and may even have been, at the outset, the result of the force of circumstances rather than free choice. Performance texts composed by professional speech writers (*logographoi*) begin to appear in the last quarter of the fifth century, the earliest three in the Antiphontic corpus alongside the set of *technai* attributed to the same author. But though they differ in style and manner from the accompanying *technai* in ways one might expect, the difference is not as extreme as one would expect. Narrative and argument based on the actual circumstances of the case still play a restricted role; probability and elaborate legal and moral casuistry are developed to a degree that strikes us as odd. It is as if the writing of an actual speech for a client (a practice that was probably newer by a generation or so than the writing of *technai*) had been embarked upon only out of necessity, for the benefit of those who proved unable to make use of a simple *technē* in order to produce a speech for themselves. The result was a genre that continued to restrict itself to the generalities characteristic of *technē*, even when there was no longer any need to do so. There may even have been occasions when the actual speech was produced by minimal modification of a *technē* already on hand. This would mean less work for the seller of the speech and also, quite possibly, a product more valuable to the buyer. He could employ it on more than one occasion (litigation was a way of life in some quarters, if one can believe contemporary complaints); and he might have a better chance of reselling it to someone else when he had no further use for it himself.

In the case of more competent speakers the written text supplied may have been an incomplete one which left the simpler parts of the case—narrative of facts, for example—to the speaker's own improvisation. The frequency of speeches that survive minus everything but their proem and/or basic argument supports this suggestion, for their number fairly well precludes accidents of transmission as a sole explanation.[2]

It also looks like more than accident that the earliest elaborate narratives to survive deal with incidents of great general interest— the mutilation of the Herms in Andocides' *On the Mysteries* and the terror of the Thirty in Lysias's *Against Agoratos* and *Against Eratosthenes*. This suggests that special circumstances were required to make a speech writer's text expand significantly on the *technē* model. Less interesting narratives may well have been presented just as extensively in the courtroom, but there would have been nothing to justify the trouble of writing them down, whether before or after delivery, with eventual publication in mind.

Some of the gaps between spoken and written versions of a speech may, of course, have been imposed by the conditions under which trials took place. The speaker who appeared second in any case might be obliged to reply to charges or supporting documents and testimony of whose exact character he knew nothing until a few minutes before he began to speak, and this would mean that the written text he memorized would have to place a premium on arguments that would hold good regardless of the new complexion the specifics of a case might assume from one moment to the next.

Yet the very fact that the system was never basically altered, and that even the practice of writing down depositions and making them available for inspection by both parties beforehand is not attested earlier than the 380s,[3] is itself an indication of the slowness with which the Athenians moved toward full utilization of the new medium of performance texts precomposed and memorized.

Isaeus, in the second quarter of the fourth century, seems to be the first orator all of whose surviving works are clearly intended for actual delivery (by clients) rather than practice or display, and Demosthenes the first one who regularly wrote and delivered his own speeches from memory. The rhetorician Alcidamas, probably writing in the decade during which the earliest Demosthenic orations were composed, provides testimony to the fact that one of the essential requirements for the success of a written speech was that it sound as if it had been improvised (B XXII 15.13).[4] If he is right, the frequency of such speeches in Demosthenes and his contemporaries is a fair indication of the point in time at which the ability to make written oratorical texts suggest an oral performance finally began to be widespread. Without that ability, there would have been no reason for an orator, even a talented one, to write out his own speeches at all; and the vast majority of those that survive, down to the middle of the century, are in fact compositions for others: men whose limited abilities left them no choice but to make use of a written text.

It does not follow, of course, that what was written down was in fact identical with the verbatim transcript of an improvisation, or that Demosthenes wrote the way Pericles talked. Acquiring the ability to make a memorized speech sound extemporaneous meant that the orator's imitation of oral composition could be more varied, more inventive, more intensely and movingly "real" than reality itself. Yet if we possessed verbatim transcripts of a Periclean oration they might well sound more like Demosthenes at points than Antiphon. Try to imagine in Antiphontic, or even Thucydidean, prose the Olympian thundering and lightning (Aristophanes, *Acharnians* 531–32) that threw all Greece into turmoil once Pericles decreed that vengeance should be wreaked upon the Megarians.

History has a more complicated pedigree and one that is harder to trace because of the almost total disappearance of the works involved. Yet later critics are unanimous in maintaining that the dominant fourth-century tradition developed under the influence of Isocrates and so, ultimately, from *technai* of an epideictic or deliberative character—not the performance text of Herodotus, or the reference texts of the Atthidographers and the Ionian chroniclers, or the hybrid work of Thucydides (discussed in chapter 6). The model speech of praise or blame, whether for an individual or, as in the Athenian *epitaphios logos*, a group or an entire city, persists into the fourth century, sometimes unaltered, sometimes combined with elements of philosophical dialogue (Xenophon's *Cyropaedia*) or actual biography (the *Evagoras* of Isocrates or the *Agesilaus* of Xenophon). The amount of detail included in texts that touched on historical themes would naturally tend to increase as written versions of real as well as model encomia began to make their appearance (the funeral speech of Hyperides, for example, the latest of the six surviving specimens of the genre and, significantly, the only one certain to have been delivered on an actual occasion). And the same would occur once *technai* designed to serve as models for symbouleutic eloquence (such as the work of Thrasymachus mentioned in chapter 5) had begun to evolve into the political pamphlets of Isocrates. The latter are still referred to on occasion as *technai*,[5] but they were also intended to be direct contributions to the formation of public opinion and so read for the same reason as one would attend an actual debate on public policy. Encomiastic and political publications of this sort can pass over fairly easily into historiography devoted primarily to giving a moral or political evaluation of individuals, institutions, and events; and such evaluations probably played a central role in the histories composed by Isocrates' students.[6] The genre was already on the way to achieving the intimate fusion of narrative and rhetorical *exempla* characteristic of works composed in Hellenistic and post-Hellenistic times, but not of those outside the *technē* tradition: Herodotus, Xenophon, and the narrative sections of Thucydides.

The style Isocrates developed and his students took over was believed by later critics to be more appropriate to written than spoken discourse. But this judgment is probably a relative one, based on a comparison with the manner of Plato or, in oratory, Isocrates' successors in the second half of the fourth century. By contrast with the masters of fifth-century prose Isocrates seems to possess more of a "podium" manner than a written one. In its attention to euphony, to leisurely development of ideas in a clear and balanced way, and to excluding anything in syntax or vocabulary that might strike a jarring note with the overall impression of orderly respectability, this manner does succeed in capturing an entire oral experience—as, presumably, Isocrates himself intended (note his own reference [12.2] to "antitheses, parallelisms, and the other devices by which one shines in public performance and which cause an audience to take notice and applaud"). But the experience is one of listening to an academic lecturer at some fairly sedate gathering, not a session of dialectic or public debate. And it represents an intermediate stage through which history passes in order to reach, in the third century, a point comparable to that reached by oratory and philosophical dialogue in the fourth. The style of Duris and his followers, the inaugurators of the so-called tragic or Peripatetic historiography of the Hellenistic age, is explicitly characterized by later critics as more suggestive of oral discourse than that of Isocrates, presumably because it embodied further departures from the original manner of deliberative or epideictic *technē*: varied, colorful narrative and—in speeches or in rhetorical insertions of authorial comment—a greater approximation to the excitement of assembly debates and the pathos and passion of courtroom appeals.[7]

It is of course in Plato (using the prose of the perfected Socratic dialogue for his illustrative models) and in Aristotle (using Isocrates and his contemporaries for the same purpose) that the notion of rhetoric is first clearly attested. This fact is in itself a strong argument in favor of the causal relationship suggested at the end of the last chapter. Until written communication had appropriated to itself a range of effects commensurate with those available to the best oral performances, and until it had ceased to be content with reproducing, in compressed, reusable form, elements excerpted from the flow of oral speech, it would have been hard to focus attention on the whole orchestration of means that constitutes the province of rhetoric or, through close comparison of works composed for different occasions, to study the way in which totally different deployments of means could serve to transmit the same message. A written *technē* that functions as a constant element in the various oral *logoi* produced on the basis of it facilitates—or better, perhaps, makes possible—the later notion of a single content given various rhetorical embodiments (see chapter 6). But as long as the embodiments continued to be oral, there would continue to be a crucial gap between written model and what was finally uttered on a specific occasion; and with nothing to fill this gap there would be nothing for the rhetorician's analytical metalanguage to work with. This is provided only when the entire speech becomes a verbal "artifact" whose composition can be followed from inception to delivery, through all its successive drafts and revisions: the whole process of "manipulating this way and that, pasting together and taking apart" (Plato, *Phaedr.* 278c9–e1), "correcting at length and at one's leisure, bringing ideas together from the works of the earlier authors one has access to and imitating their felicities, introducing improvements at the suggestion of friends and, after repeated scrutiny of one's own, purifying and rewriting . . . slowly, fashioning one's own discourse and adjusting the parts exactly and harmoniously to each other with deliberate thought" (Alcidamas B XXII 15.4 and 16).[8]

These two descriptions, the earliest ones surviving in Greek of the process of careful written composition, are also from the two earliest writers in whom the word *rhetoric* is attested (for Alcidamas, 15.1). And both writers, though convinced that the ability to do such composition is of limited value to the prospective speaker, are obviously experts at it themselves. Alcidamas admits as much (15.29–32); for Plato, if the dialogues themselves are not evidence enough, there is the famous story (Dion. Hal., *De comp. verb.* 25, Quintilian 8.6.64) of the different versions of the opening sentence of the *Republic* that Plato left under his pillow on the day he died: busily engaged, it would seem, in the process of "manipulating this way and that, pasting together and taking apart" right up to the end.

Until such expertise had been obtained, however, one suspects that even the fundamental rhetorical category of style (*lexis*) would have been difficult to disentangle from that of delivery. The two are still closely associated by Isocrates when in his epistle to Philip (5.25–27) he first complains of the letter writer's general inability to make use of the persuasive techniques available to the oral performer, then goes on, in almost the same breath, to speak of his decision in the present instance to forgo "stylistic harmonies and ornaments" (*tais peri tēn lexin eurythmiais kai poikiliais*) as well. These are seen as adding to the persuasiveness of a discourse in the same way as intonation (*phōnē*), the speaker's earnestness (*spoudē*) and feel for the occasion (*kairoi*), and the impression of him (*doxa*) which the projection of his character (*ēthos*) creates on an audience. Even more strikingly, in what is the earliest surviving attempt to isolate *lexis* as a separate subject of inquiry (*Rhet.* 3.1), Aristotle introduces it in close conjunction with a discussion of delivery (*hypokrisis*), noting the parallel ways in which prizes are bestowed upon orations and poems because of their delivery and upon written speeches because of their style (1404a15–19). It is as if he could only define style and illustrate its importance as a factor in written composition by a kind of analogy.[9] What delivery (the way a particular performer renders a poetic or oratorical text) is to an entire oral presentation and its success with an audience, such is style to a piece into whose presentation the factor of delivery does not enter. The performer delivers the whole text of his role to the audience; and, in corresponding fashion, style "delivers" the contents of the role into a written text. It is, to use the expression of a modern critic, a kind of "writing out loud" ("écrire à haute voix"), the written word's effort to do the work of the spoken word.[10]

The art of "writing out loud" did not, however, develop in a vacuum, out of a simple desire to explore the possibilities of a new medium, and with the unexpected result that, at a fairly late stage in the process, a basis for sophisticated rhetorical analysis came into being for the first time. Deliberate search for a surer, more effective, more controllable method of written communication than that provided by fifth-century *technē* was probably a decisive consideration from the start.

Confronted with clients of only moderate abilities, professional speech writers were compelled, as they would not have been in composing for themselves or for gifted students, to produce a written text that might suggest the real person, real moral commitment (*prohairesis*), and real character (*ēthos*) behind the words it contained. In this way they were contributing to the development of a medium so successful for projecting another person before an audience that orators eventually decided to use it for self-projection as well.

Plato and Isocrates, the one disqualified by conviction and the other by physical disabilities from the direct role in political life they might otherwise have been expected to play, were left with the alternative of seeking to make an impact on their contemporaries through teaching or writing. And it was only the reading text, whether or not conceived as a reproduction of a single actual performance, that could serve their purposes.

It is thus no accident that both writers, when addressing themselves explicitly to questions of literary and rhetorical analysis, lay particular stress on the shortcomings of the nonreading, multiperformance text (i.e., the *technē*) and the means for overcoming them. The famous passage (*Phaedr.* 274b6–78e2) usually known as Plato's attack on the written "word" is, in the first instance, an attack on the written *technē*. For it is written *technē*, not simply any piece of writing, that is particularly vulnerable to the Platonic charge (276b1–77a4) of being an inadequate substitute for instruction based on close association between teacher and student; and it is written *technē* whose inability to answer questions about its own meaning or defend itself from attacks (275d4–e5) is most likely to lead to dangerous misinterpretation. Misinterpretation is something *technē* not only allows but actually invites—by leaving entirely to the student the choice of which one among the various arguments it presents to use and when. What is not always clear to us was probably perfectly clear to Plato's contemporaries and immediate followers. The author of the *Seventh Letter,* at any rate, has no doubt as to what sort of written text Plato had primarily in mind. In a clear echo of the entire discussion of writing in the *Phaedrus,* he attacks the younger Dionysius for thinking he had in his possession a book which "as if it were a *technē*" (341b2–5) incorporated the essence of Platonic philosophy.

Plato's response to such inadequacies was twofold: first, the foundation of the Academy and, with it, a tradition of metalinguistic commentary and oral instruction that would guarantee authenticity to the version of his doctrine received by his direct successors and, presumably, check the erosion of the powers of memory to which excessive use of writing led (cf. *Phaedr.* 275a–b); second, the creation, through the Platonic dialogue, of a written medium that would, especially in its more dramatic, "Socratic" moments, be free from as many as possible of the defects to which earlier written texts were subject.

A Socratic dialogue, unlike a *technē,* is regularly linked to a particular situation, sometimes (as in the *Symposium,* the *Theaetetus,* and the *Parmenides*) by way of an elaborate introductory fiction explaining how the details of a particular conversation came to be known to the putative narrator. One is rarely offered, as one regularly is in a *technē,* an argument out of context. The contrast is intentionally emphasized in the *Phaedrus,* where the first thing Socrates does in his restatement of Lysias's attack on love (a typical *technē*) is to assign it to a specific speaker and a specific occasion: the restatement is to be understood as the effort on the part of a lover to advance his suit by pretending to be a nonlover (see chapter 1). One possible path of misinterpretation is thereby shut off from the outset; and the dramatic setting makes it clear that readers must proceed along any such path—or set of paths—with a certain amount of caution. They will thus see the contrast between, say, the case for resistance and the case for conformity to the demands of a hostile community and its laws as something less confrontational and more complex once it ceases to be a Sophistic antilogy and becomes the two acts entitled *Apology* and *Crito* in the drama of the Last Days of Socrates.

The dramatic form also excludes the presence of any single voice of authority. Even Socrates himself, though his moral and intellectual stature and the character of his whole life make anything he says worth listening to, is not a completely reliable spokesman for the author. There is always the possibility of *ad hominem* arguments, or arguments accepted in one dialogue to be rejected or ignored in another, or arguments offered as tentative suggestions rather than firm conclusions. And Plato is at no pains to conceal the existence of such discrepancies. What does emerge as the author's message—with a clarity and certainty impossible in a *technē*—is the crucial importance of the dialectical method itself, whose use never varies from situation to situation, and the basic validity of those Socratic positions that stand the test of repeated propounding and examination. Like the only sort of written text Plato explicitly approves of (*Phaedr.* 278b8–d6), the corpus of Socratic dialogues bears witness to the author's ability to replace anything in it with something better should need arise—in the form of new evidence, new insights, new arguments not envisioned when the original piece was produced.

The situation is completely different with the typical *technē*—designed for use on repeated occasions, and composed of generalities that are easily mistaken for universally valid statements and often appear alongside competing generalities every bit as valid (or invalid). Such a text almost inevitably claims to be more than it is and tends to be taken for more than it claims to be. The labor of selecting and eliminating, cutting and pasting, that goes into its preparation is thus a fit subject for ridicule. The only true transmission of an entire "art" is, in Plato's view, that which involves, not a set of selected samples, but all the metalanguage which explains how those samples are arrived at. And this is much too complex a thing for inclusion in any one set of written documents. The Socratic dialogue, on the other hand, is sufficiently "occasional" in its character to justify the painstaking adjustment of the last trope and figure into their proper places—suitably temporary means to the temporary aspect of the persuasive, or "psychagogic," end that the principal interlocutor has in mind.

Plato's attack is probably a defense as well. There were doubtless those who interpreted his rejection of demonstration texts in favor of reading texts as proof of an inability to improvise one's own speech on the basis of a *technē*—rather than, as was true in Plato's case, of a desire to discourage others from such improvisation. Inability to improvise is one of the charges his contemporary Alcidamas brings (*On the Sophists*, 9–13) against those whose reputation is based primarily on the polish of their published works; and there is no reason to believe that, as often suggested, Isocrates was the only object of Alcidamas's attack. In the *Phaedrus* Plato turns the argument around, interpreting the publication of demonstration texts as proof of an inability even to conceive, much less improvise, something better on one's own—rather than, as was true in the case of most *technē* writers, of a desire to *encourage* others to come up with such improvisation. Isocrates makes a similar rejoinder, in a series of passages that have obviously influenced, or been influenced by, the more famous one in the *Phaedrus*, and which, even more clearly than their Platonic counterparts, are the work of someone who was himself open to attack for too much reliance on the written word. True eloquence—a product of natural talent, practice, and familiarity with earlier oratory—is contrasted with the rudimentary achievements based on mastery of *topoi* or, as Isocrates calls them, *ideai* (13.16, 15.183). As constant ingredients in all discourse, these *topoi* represent the only part of the discipline which can be mastered with exact knowledge (*epistēmē*: 13.16, 15.185 and 271) or precision (*akribeia*: 15.190)—hence, presumably, the only part which can be inculcated through the written teaching models of whose shortcomings Isocrates complains at 13.12–13 (see chapter 5) and 19. At the same time it is perfectly clear that, in Isocrates' view, true eloquence can be written as well as oral; and—like Plato—he is deeply committed to the production of such eloquence. In justifying this commitment both authors take over the inherited contrast between written *technē* and oral performance and turn it into a contrast between *technē* and finished performance text—the written reproduction or re-creation (for a reading public, presumably) of a real or imaginary oral occasion.[11]

Isocrates' re-creations of such occasions are far less effective than Plato's—a result of his having made far less progress toward mastering the art of writing out loud. There is also a correspondingly greater reluctance to accept the claims of the new analytic and prescriptive technique first broached as a possibility in the *Phaedrus*. *Technē* is treated as something suspect for intrinsic reasons, not simply because of the limitations to which existing versions of it are subject. On the other hand, Isocrates' educational program shows clear signs of having been evolved during the course of the same sort of conscious effort at transcending those limitations as is attested in Plato. Socrates at the end of the *Phaedrus* (279a3–b2) acknowledges the existence of a certain element of philosophy (*tis philosophia*) in Isocrates' make-up; and the whole dialogue, by virtue of the way it takes over and extends certain procedures used earlier in Isocrates' *Helen* and *Busiris* is a striking testimony both to the existence and to the limitations of Isocratean "philosophy" as applied to the realm of discourse.[12]

The basic plan of all three works is identical: first, criticism of a particular piece of fifth- or early fourth-century *technē*: Lysias's attack on love, Polycrates' encomium of Busiris, Gorgias's defense of Helen; then, a text that treats the same subject in what the author believes to be proper fashion.[13] Both criticisms, moreover, reveal the same basic discontent with one of the basic principles of early *technē*. To be acceptable, praise and blame must involve—as they do not in *technē*—taking a particular stand on the basis of universal principles to which an author is willing to commit himself. Love and Helen are both divine beings and any speech concerning them must accordingly be a speech praising their virtues—not one that finds fault (Lysias) or offers what purports to be praise but is in fact an excuse for shortcomings (Gorgias). Criticism of love is only allowable in the specific context of the pretended nonlover's indirect wooing, and within a larger argument that makes clear the difference between true love and its debased counterpart. Helen's defense must refer only to those particular attributes (beauty, descent from the highest gods, attractiveness to a hero of the stature of Theseus) and achievements (unification of Greece in common cause against the barbarians) whose desirability in all situations can be taken for granted.[14] The dangers inherent in Gorgias's general condonation of acts committed under any sort of constraint (discussed in chapter 5) or Lysias's condemnation of all irrational psychological states are thereby avoided. Finally, both authors have rejected the single most serious formal limitation on *technē*. The core of instruction is still a model piece showing the student what to do, but the piece is contrasted with another showing what *not* to do; and this requires a considerable use of language talking about language if the author is to make clear why one piece is good and the other bad.

Plato, however, overcomes these formal limitations much more completely than does Isocrates. His critical exposition is more extensive, more explicit, and more wide-ranging: concerned with argumentation, diction, arrangement, and overall artistic unity as well as with the essentially moral considerations that occupy Isocrates. The contrast here is almost as striking as that between, on the one hand, Plato's flamboyant rhetoric, with its dithyrambic style, intricate, idiosyncratic arrangement, and brilliantly mythologized psychology and epistemology, and, on the other hand, Isocrates' often irrelevant, occasionally idealized or censored, but basically sober catalogue of the virtues that should be ascribed to Helen.

Outside the *Helen* and *Busiris*, Isocrates' criticism ranges somewhat more widely, touching occasionally (4.9, 9.8–10, 15.46–47) on the way subject matter (*praxeis, hypothesis*) is to be treated at the level of both thought (*enthymēmata*) and diction (*lexis, onomata*). More often, however, he reduces the two processes to the single one of arriving at a proper choice of "types" (*eidē, ideai*) of oratorical procedure (12.2, 13.16–17), or obscures their distinction as part of some vaguer antithesis.[15] Moreover, presentation is almost always seen as serving the single overriding purpose of making familiar but major facts and ideas seem new and varied enough to hold the attention of an audience (2.41, 4.8–10, 5.93, 10.11–13, 12.34–36). There is no counterpart—either here or in the Isocratean formulation that is partially taken over for the definition of rhetoric in the *Phaedrus* (cf. Thompson's note on 261a7–b3)—to the Platonic idea of multiple correlations between different types of audience and different means of presenting a single message.

One further "non-Isocratean" feature of the *Phaedrus* deserves mention. It is less striking than those already mentioned, though of equal significance for Plato's position in the development of rhetorical theory. As if to underline the close interconnection between the analysis of persuasion and the availability of actual samples of persuasion in written form, Socrates insists on having Lysias "himself" present—in the form of a verbatim reading of the text of his *technē*. He will not settle for the oral epideixis of its content that Phaedrus was first intending to provide (227d6–e2). Isocrates, on the other hand, had contented himself, both in the *Helen* and the *Busiris,* with a simple summary of those points in the work of his predecessors he found unsatisfactory. Neither here, nor anywhere else in his published works, does he give a verbatim record of another author's writing. Plato's procedure is the more innovative: yet another instance of his moving away from the protorhetorical conception of *technē* as, above all, a selection of imitable instances of the skill of its author.[16] The final break with the tradition, however, only comes with Aristotle, who provides no instances of his own skill at all, confining himself to analysis and, when examples are required, to excerpts from the published writings of others.

This final break was probably the decisive one as well. The reading text is fundamental to rhetoric, and no author can simply "read" a text that he himself has composed. He will always be to some extent recalling it, and memory interferes with analysis. It resuscitates the spontaneous, improvisational aspects of the creative process, and thereby increases the difficulty of viewing a text as generated through self-conscious application of explicitly formulated principles with the demands of a particular situation in mind. Aristotle's procedural innovation is not simply a minor refinement, nor even a side effect of his basic approach. It must have been something of which he was fully and continuously aware. The plethora of borrowed examples found in the *Rhetoric* is obviously the product of the same sort of extensive study as preceded the publication of his other main work on the subject, the *Compendium of Techniques (Synagōgē technōn).* The exact character of this comprehensive epitome of the work of all of Aristotle's predecessors in the writing of *technai* can only be surmised from the scant fragments of it which remain.[17] If, however, as has been argued here, the epitomized texts consisted mainly of sample speeches or speech parts, producing a compendium would be an undertaking almost exactly comparable to what lies behind the citations in the *Rhetoric:* first a selection of excerpts representing each of the procedures illustrated in earlier *technē,* and then a presentation of the material thus collected in accordance with some classificatory scheme of the author's own devising—presumably more exhaustive, complete and systematic than anything found in his sources. The only difference would be that the works excerpted for the *Rhetoric* could have included performance texts as well as *technai.* But the vast majority of written texts available in the middle years of the century would have been either *technai* or performance texts published, like *technai,* for prospective users rather than prospective readers.

It was probably at this point, in the course of seeking a satisfactory scheme of classification, that the "canonical" arrangement of the judicial oration became part of the tradition—partially by accident, partially by design. An incipient ordering is evident in the earliest surviving testimony (Plato, *Phaedr.* 266d5–67d4) to the existence, already within the Academy, of the sort of drive toward collection and arrangement that was to culminate in Aristotle's *Compendium:*

> *Phaedrus:* And very numerous they are, Socrates [the "nondialectical" parts of rhetoric], those found in the books on *logōn technē.*
>
> *Socrates:* Thanks for reminding me: the proem to begin with, I imagine—how it ought to be delivered at the start of the speech. This is what you mean, right—the finer refinements (*ta kompsa*) of the art.
>
> *Phaedrus:* Yes.
>
> *Socrates:* And second, obviously some sort of narrative (*diēgēsis*), and witness depositions on top of that; third, evidence and signs; fourth, probabilities; and proofs (*pisteis*), I think, and supplementary proofs are mentioned, at least by that *non-pareil* of word craftsmen, the gentleman from Byzantium.
>
> *Phaedrus:* You mean Theodorus—admirable man.

Socrates: Who else? And refutation and supplementary refutation, how it should be conducted in both prosecution and defense . . . [There follows an extensive list of procedures and their "discoverers"]. . . . And as for the conclusion of the speech, I assume there is general agreement that there should be one, some calling it recapitulation (*epanodos*), and others something else.

It is easy to assume (and often is assumed) that the ordering of items in this list is both traditional—a replica of the way the items would appear in a typical *technē*—and chronological, a replica of what would be found in a typical speech.[18] In fact, however, it is nowhere explicitly stated that the arrangement is traditional rather than of Socrates' own devising; and the implied "chronological" organizing principle breaks down after the second item in the list, to reappear briefly at the end. The apparent randomness of the intervening section may well have been more in keeping with the original notion of *technē* as a listing and illustration of the basic components or divisions (*merē*) of discourse (*logos*). Given the multivalence of the term *logos,* the "parts" involved might have been, among other things, proem, narrative and the like (*logos* thought of as a particular speech); wish, command, question and answer (*logos* as sentence type, see Protagoras B III 10); verb, noun, and the other categories still known as "parts" of speech (*logos* as syntactical element); or dicanic, symbouleutic, and epideictic oratory (*logos* as public speaking in general). Items from any or all of these categories might have appeared in the table of contents of a typical *technē*—in such a way as to exclude the imposition of any single scheme of arrangement, be it traditional or chronological.

The chronological principle, insofar as it is felt as a determining consideration in the ordering of items in Socrates' list, is best taken as Plato's own innovation. The whole notion of a proper, inevitable order of presentation with first things first, last things last, and all things in well-proportioned and fixed relationship to each other, whether they are the parts of an oration or the limbs of a human body is typically Platonic (*Phaedr.* 263c2–5). Lack of such an order is accordingly prime grounds for faulting Lysias: there is, Socrates complains (264a4–e3), no discernible reason why any of the constituent parts of his speech should come before or after any other part. Having made this point, he goes on—rather oddly if one accepts the traditional interpretation of 266d5 ff.—to criticize a *technē* organized around the very principle of proper ordering of parts of whose absence he has just been complaining.

If the ordering is Socrates' own contribution, however, his procedure is more understandable. He is simply presenting the content of earlier *technē* in what is—from his point of view—the most favorable possible light. Proper ordering in an oration must, of course, be a consideration subordinate to proper dialectical reasoning; and any *technē* centered around external (that is, non-dialectical) matters is deeply flawed from the start. But there is no reason why such a *technē* need to be totally useless: it can still point out, at least in a general way, the principal virtue of a good exterior, which is to call attention and make more accessible the interior for whose sake it exists. Every proper speech has a definite message to communicate and so a natural beginning, middle, and end. The speaker will, in the normal course of things, announce his subject before starting (proem), state the facts of his case (*diēgēsis*) before attempting to infer anything from them (*pisteis*), and finally, since a speech must end at some point (no disagreement about that!) give a brief reminder (*epanodos*) of what has been said just before the end comes. The order of procedure is an obvious one, but precisely for that reason it is an order whose value even Lysias and his likes ought to be able to understand—if they can be cured of their self-importance and preoccupation with the showy and exotic, and if they can be persuaded to take stock of what their *technē* amounts to with the modicum of Socratic order and clarity that the survey of 266d ff. seeks to introduce.

The order and clarity become even more evident once Plato's list is taken over, in simplified form, as a basis for the section (3.13–19) of Aristotle's *Rhetoric* devoted to the topic of arrangement. There the number of essential "parts" is reduced to four: proem, narrative, proof, and epilogue and they are discussed in the order in which they would necessarily appear in any speech. Less evident, though still clearer than in Plato, is the degree to which this arrangement is and is not traditional. Aristotle obviously regards arrangement as the sort of subject with which protorhetoric had been largely concerned: basically, those subjects that are peripheral to the main issue (*ta exō tou pragmatos: Rhet.* 1.1 1354b16–19) or directed at audience response (*ta pros ton akroatēn:* 3.14 1415a1–2, b7–8 and 34–36) or concerned with the composition of individual parts of an oration rather than the role those parts should play in achieving the orator's overall purpose (*ti dei to prooimion ē tēn diēgēsin echein:* 1.1 1354b18–19). But it is made equally obvious that this tetrad is simpler than what was usually found in earlier *technē:* it is a kind of compromise between Aristotle's own conviction that the only indispensable and constant parts of a speech are statement of subject matter and proof (3.13 1414a31–37, b7–8) and the proliferation of "parts" recognized by most of his predecessors. Aristotle discusses many of those parts, but treats other possible orderings of them as inferior alternatives to, or pointless refinements on, his own. The result is, perhaps for the first time, a list confined to the maximum number of parts that can be expected to appear in every type of speech (3.13 1414b8–9). It is always possible to construct an oration that begins with a proem followed, in order, by narrative, proof, and epilogue. The fact is an obvious one; but Aristotle is here following Plato in regarding the obvious as something which earlier *technē* might seek but which was just barely within the range of possibility for it to achieve.

Having once emerged in this fashion through the work of collecting and excerpting, the tetrad became a standard part of rhetorical theory, exercising in turn a continuing influence on practice, whether or not it was used, as it is in *Rhetoric* 3, as a means of organizing material drawn extensively from the work of one's predecessors. The same retrospective, doxographical perspective seems, however, to have been present in the one other early work in which the tetrad is known to have appeared, the *technē* of Theodectes. There can be little doubt about the generally Aristotelian character of this treatise. Its contents, as known from later citations, are paralleled often enough in *Rhetoric* 3 that some scholars believed it to be the same book. Others follow Valerius Maximus (8.14.3) in making it a different version of the same material, "Theodectean" in the same way as the different versions of Aris-

133

totle's ethics are Nicomachean and Eudemian.[19] Whatever the exact connection, there are several good reasons for believing it to have been a compendium. The author of the spurious Aristotelian letter preceding the *Rhetorica ad Alexandrum* writes of having incorporated into his own work "whatever choice contributions other treatise writers have made to the subject in their own works" and cites two sources for his information: a treatise of his own, written for (or dedicated to) Theodectes, and the *technē* of Corax (1421a38–b3 = 4.22–5.1 Fuhrmann). It follows, since Corax as initiator of the whole tradition could hardly have borrowed from other writers, that the Theodectean work *did* collect such material from other sources, or was regarded by the author of the letter as having done so.

The same inference should perhaps be drawn from the item in the ancient list of the writings of Aristotle which reads, in some manuscripts of one version of the list, "The single book of the compendium of the art of Theodectes." This means either Aristotle's own compendium of Theodectes' work or—more likely, since there would be no reason for epitomizing Theodectes apart from the other *technai* that appeared in the *Synagōgē technōn*—Theodectes' compendium of the art (of rhetoric).[20] Aristotle himself seems to have a work of collection in mind when he refers the reader to "the Theodectean writings" (*ta Theodekteia*) for "a fairly complete enumeration of the way periods can begin" (*Rhet.* 3.8 1410b2–3). What is involved is evidently a cataloguing of typical sentence openings similar to the collection of typically constructed cola (all drawn from Isocrates' *Panegyricus*) in the paragraph that immediately precedes in Aristotle's text. And both catalogues must be a product of the same sort of excerpting and classifying of material contained in earlier texts that underlies *Rhetoric* 3.13–19, the *Synagōgē*, and, incipiently, the brief survey in the *Phaedrus*.

Finally, there is the reference to Theodectes in the comic poet Antiphanes' acid comment (fr. 113 Kock) on the unseemly after-dinner dancing of a polymath who can "explain Heraclitus so that all can understand, has by his own unaided efforts (*monos*) discovered (or "invented": *hēure*) the *technē* of Theodectes and compiled summaries of all the plays of Euripides."[21] It is not clear how anyone other than its author could invent or discover a *technē*—perhaps by thinking of it independently, perhaps by having been, or claiming to have been, the person wrongly deprived of credit for the discovery. But the implications of *monos* are less ambiguous. If doing a thing single-handedly is a feat to be mentioned alongside popularizing Heraclitus and mastering the whole content of Euripides, the thing referred to is likely to be one for which the credit is normally shared among a number of people.[22] And in the present context this can hardly be anything but a *technē* that synthesizes, or excerpts from, the achievements of many writers. Praise (or ridicule) someone for expounding relativity to the layman, preparing didascalia for all of Lope de Vega, and being a one-man Pauly-Wissowa, and the encomium will be sufficient grounds for concluding, even when the work in question is irretrievably lost, that the Pauly-Wissowa was a collective enterprise.

It is impossible to know how much of the enterprise was Aristotelian and how much Theodectean. The correspondences with *Rhetoric* 3 point to the existence of unacknowledged borrowings of an extensiveness unparalleled elsewhere in Aristotle unless we assume that he regarded the *Theodekteia* as, in some important sense, his own work. A simple explanation, though not the only possible one, is that Aristotle provided the basic categories, drawn from a fairly cursory survey of the tradition, and that Theodectes, whose memory was to become proverbial (Cicero, *Tusc.* 1.59; Quintilian 11.2.51; Aelian, *An. Hist.* 6.10b) did the actual excerpting and classifying.

Whatever the exact relationship, the ancient reports linking Theodectes to Isocrates as well as to Aristotle do not justify the usual assumption of an Isocratean origin for the quadripartite arrangement that is common to Aristotle and Theodectes. Quadripartition itself (unparalleled in Isocrates, but reminiscent of Aristotle's four causes, four elements, four types of democracy, and three or four basic modes of syllogism) argues against this, as does the doxographical purpose to which it is put—notoriously an Aristotelian, not an Isocratean concern. Also Aristotelian in character are the fairly clear "prescriptive" elements attested for Theodectes, which may represent, along with the quadripartite doxography, a new departure in the *technē* tradition. Each speech part has its proper goal (*telos:* fr. 133), set of tasks (*erga:* fr. 134), and excellences (*aretai:* fr. 126), just as the sentence has its appropriate rhythms (frs. 128–29). The importance assigned to these qualities was probably inferred and/or exemplified from earlier orations and *technai* rather than discussed or defended at length: brevity as a virtue of narrative, for example, from the frequency of a certain type of opening formula ("Now I shall set forth the facts of the case as briefly as I can"),[23] and the necessity of completeness and chronological order from similar recurring statements of a programmatic character.[24] Even so, however, their presence, like the idea of an exhaustive classification of rhetorical parts itself, seems decidedly un-Isocratean. It is incompatible both with the extremely vague, unsystematic habit of mind revealed in his writings and with the frequency of the passages in those writings that deny the possibility of reducing eloquence to the rules of art at all.

Theodectes' association with Isocrates, if it existed, was probably a personal and/or literary one. It may have contributed to the belief—questioned even in antiquity—that Isocrates himself wrote a general *technē* organized along the line of Theodectes'. It may also—assuming that Theodectes drew heavily on his friend's work for the examples in his compendium—account for the frequency with which Isocrates is cited in Aristotle's *Rhetoric* (more often than any author except Homer). But the so-called Isocratean rhetorical treatise organized around a discussion of proem, narrative, proof, and epilogue rather than the classification by subject matter found in Aristotle's *Rhetoric* is, at most, the "Theodectean" treatise; and the one format may well be, in its own way, as Aristotelian as the other.[25]

Whether, as is quite possible, Aristotle's own *Synagōgē* was also Theodectean in plan will doubtless never be known. Whatever its plan, it takes its place alongside *Rhet.* 3.13–19, the *Theodekteia,* and the survey passage from the *Phaedrus* already discussed as a striking testimony to the prominence that the whole process of "bringing ideas together from the works of earlier authors" and "imitating their felicities" had come to occupy—in the theory as well as the practice of Attic prose in the middle years of the fourth century.

Writer and theoretician alike are, above all, readers, and reading is now an operation of scanning and collecting (cf. Latin *legere*), not the recalling to mind and recognition that the Greek word (*anagignōskein*), coined a century or more earlier, had originally designated.

The "historical" context thus created for the study both of style and, more generally, the entire process of rhetorical communication was, in some sense, a tribute to the actual historical process by which a consciousness of style had come into being. To be aware of style was, inevitably, to be aware of the gradual series of accretions by which the practice and demonstration text of the late fifth century had become a rhetorically effective reading text. Style was thus conceived as a matter of process and precedent—by contrast with the timelessness of dialectic—so that the historical approach had the further effect of confirming the essential, but essentially subordinate, position that rhetoric assigned and continued to assign to manner as against matter.

Logōn technē had dominated the writing of prose for more than a generation during a critical formative period in its history, and had virtually excluded from texts written during that period anything not of a general nature and permanent significance. The result was a relegation of all other aspects of composition to a subordinate status from which they were never really to emerge. Even rhetoric, for all its preoccupation with the particular means required to adjust a message to a given occasion, does not alter this situation. It continues to think in terms of exemplifications, illustrations, and variations; and these are related to general principles in somewhat the same way that, at an earlier period, individual items in an actual speech would have been related to the written *technē* from which they were generated. The resultant ordering of the author's tasks is as much chronological as hierarchical. Rhetorical discussions of the art of composition, stressing as they do the way general principles should be prior to specific instance, substance to form, fundamental message to the various ploys and strategies taken to put it across in a given situation, simply call for a reenactment of the process by which the specifically rhetorical or reading text came into being.[26]

Ontogeny recapitulates phylogeny, so it would seem, in literary and rhetorical as well as biological genesis. But the parallel must not be pressed too far. Rhetoric's priorities were influenced, not completely determined, by the historical circumstances of its origin. Primacy of substance over form owes at least as much to the radically new character Platonic and Aristotelian philosophy gave to the prospective author's attitude toward his subject matter. The shape in which the discipline of rhetoric ultimately crystallized cannot be understood without some consideration of the way the two philosophers' views of eloquence and poetry were the result of a desire to make both arts the chosen instruments for transmitting the particular sort of messages they considered most important.

Eight

Rhetoric and Philosophy

One of the results of the transformation of the character of written prose discussed in the last chapter was the creation of a body of reading texts comparable to the performance texts that had existed at a rather earlier date for poetry. And this in turn made possible—given the decreasing importance of performance in securing an audience for poetry—the assimilation of prose and poetic texts as complementary parts of a single literary heritage. Earlier poetry ceases to play a vital role in this heritage to the degree that it falls below the minimum level that will allow a performance text to function as an effective reading text as well; and new prose fails to acquire such a role to the degree that it fails to stay well above it. The process of assimilation is reflected in, and partially determines, the development of Platonic and Aristotelian rhetoric—a new discipline intended to provide a general vehicle for the dissemination of certain types of philosophical message. Plato's attacks on poets and orators for failing to transmit such messages are conducted separately in the *Gorgias* and the *Republic*—primarily with oral transmissions in mind.[1] A decade or two later they merge, in the *Phaedrus*, into a single laying down of standards all *written* discourse must meet if it is to escape condemnation; and the creation or ideation of texts that will meet such standards runs parallel during the rest of the century for poetry and prose.

What is involved in both instances is an effort to save—for the philosophical reader—the converging traditions of Greek poetry and eloquence in much the same way as the Platonic and Aristotelian doctrine of forms and causes seeks to "save" the phenomena of the perceived world from the radical critique to which they had been subjected in the preceding century.[2] Poetry and oratory can do more than make lies sound like truth. They are also means for making truth sound like truth—the only means, on many occasions, that are available. As such, they are not simply acceptable to the philosopher but necessary for his purposes. Rhetoric is the art of harnessing and focusing poetical and oratorical energy with such ends in mind.

Plato himself indicates the direction this operation of salvage and rehabilitation is to take, even in the course of the most famous and vigorous of his denunciations of the tradition. Poetry is to be permitted in the ideal state if it confines itself to hymns and encomia, or to the representation of virtuous men and noble deeds.[3] It is to be a kind of rhetorical protrepsis that inspires admiration for good qualities and good actions by linking them to the most revered figures, human and divine, of mythological and historical tradition. Isocrates takes up the suggestion and transfers it to prose—or writes with parallel concern for the rehabilitation of traditional subject matter—when he criticizes the work of his predecessors Gorgias and Polycrates (see chapter 7) in much the same way that Plato criticizes Homer. Both Isocratean critiques are followed by prose encomia intended to show how figures such as Helen and Busiris *should* be treated. The encomiast must be prepared to disregard transmitted stories about them (whether true or false) if the only alternative is to attribute shameful acts and qualities to gods and the children of gods. Similar considerations demand suppressing what is discreditable to Athens in the reworkings of historical tradition that appear in Isocrates' *Panegyricus* and Plato's *Menexenus*.[4] Elsewhere (in the *Timaeus*, *Republic*, *Phaedo*, and *Gorgias*) Plato uses motifs from, or imitations of, cosmological and eschatological poetry as a means for saying, as impressively as possible, what the creation of the universe, or the cosmic processes by which good is rewarded and evil punished, might be *like*, even though there may be other, better means available for discussing whether there actually *are* such processes and, if so, *what*, exactly, they are. The ongoing debate among Plato's successors as to the "literal" or "metaphorical" character of Plato's most famous venture into cosmogony may go back to sessions in the Academy when these other, better means were employed or contemplated.[5]

The conception of comedy presented in the *Laws* (see chapter 1) amounts to a rehabilitation of the genre, superseding or modifying the earlier critique in the *Republic*, and Aristotle began a similar rehabilitation of tragedy by insisting on the cathartic function of its appeal to the emotions and by subordinating its potentially dangerous illusionistic features to the single overriding task of offering, through *mythos*, an imitation, recognized as such by its audience, of things as they are or should be. Aristotle's successors carried the process further in the same direction by emphasizing the idealizing aspect of tragic imitation at the expense of the realistic.

Moral earnestness, combined with social and political views of a generally conservative cast, are usually seen as the motivating forces behind this work of rehabilitation. But surely the decisive consideration lay elsewhere—in the increased confidence in the human capacity for accurate understanding and communication which was an essential part of the vast Platonic and Aristotelian organization of knowledge and the means of acquiring it.

This is what would render obsolete a *technē* presenting, for example, the advantages of boldness in planning and waging a battle followed by another devoted to the contrasting values of caution, and make possible its replacement by a treatise on strategy and military discipline. The exercise of the central military virtue, bravery, can now be linked—Platonically—to a proper assessment of what is and is not to be feared; and boldness, caution, rashness, and the like can be reduced to different ways of referring to it, depending on whether the situation is one in which the possible consequences of engaging the enemy (defeat, death) are more or less to be feared than those of not engaging him (slavery, disgrace, etc.). To be practically useful, this definition must, of course, be accompanied by an accurate morphology of things to be feared. Once the possibility of such a morphology is accepted, however, along with comparable possibilities for all the subjects of military discourse, the way is open to a dialectical determination of the best thing to do in any given situation. A similar determination can also be made of all the characters and psychological states to be confronted in a speaker's audiences, and of all the reactions which are capable of being produced in each.

At this point one has achieved an exact morphology of the real (the military dialectician's province insofar as it pertains to subject matter, the rhetorician's as pertains to audience psychology). It remains to correlate its dialectical and rhetorical halves—by a study of the various types of discourse and discourse components in which subject matter can be incorporated and the reactions that each of these is capable of producing in different types of audience. This in turn enables the determination of which components will be optimally effective for the situation and audience at hand and so, finally, their combination into the discourse required (see chapter 1 for this summary of the Platonic program).

The discourse is capable, if need be, of transcription in writing; and it is difficult to see how the exact calculation of effect envisaged by Plato—or even the more approximate ones found in later rhetoricians, beginning with Aristotle—would be possible unless writing were involved in the whole process from the start. The growing sophistication of written technology in the period is a result, in part, of its usefulness in the accumulation and dissemination of the exact knowledge required for Plato's morphology of the real; and the availability, or presumed availability in some degree or other, of such knowledge distinguishes rhetoric from its antecedents as much as does its concern with the means and mechanics of presentation.

Various explanations are possible of why fifth-century writers failed to develop a true rhetoric of martial discourse, limiting themselves instead to a simple pairing of calls to boldness and calls to caution, with an implicit invitation to the student to decide which of the two is applicable, and to what extent, in various situations as they arise. Laziness, diffidence, irresponsibility, realism, relativism, and skepticism all come to mind; and all of them, in various degrees and at various times, may have played their part. None of them, however, is compatible with the existence of the sort of knowledge that rhetoric presupposes; and this is a critical factor in the failure of early *technē* to anticipate fourth-century attempts to put the communicative resources of traditional poetry and eloquence to new use. The discipline is a tentative, exploratory one. The morphology of the real with which it works is too ill defined in its boundaries and basic configurations for any part of it to serve as a solid core that could remain constant through experiments with presenting it to an audience in different ways.

In the absence of the sort of certainty about the nature of the physical, moral, and sociopolitical universe that one finds in Plato and Aristotle, it is hard even to draw a constant, clear line of division between dialectical and rhetorical modes of procedure. What seems a rhetorical metaphor can just as well be a heuristic analogy designed to extend the boundaries of knowledge; and a rhetorical overstatement may be hard to distinguish from a straightforward exhortation to transform the character of attitudes and institutions.[6] Virtuoso demonstrations extolling the virtues of salt, mud, nonlovers, unfaithful wives, and cannibalistic kings shade over into genuine intellectual paradoxes of the sort explored by the Eleatics and, later, Plato and the Stoics.[7] (The philosopher king is eulogized in what Plato terms explicitly a *para doxan* [*Rep.* 5.473e4], the idea of the Good in a *hyperbolē* [6.509c2].) The same word (*eidos, idea*) may refer to one of the basic modes of discourse (the rhetorical or dialectical topos, the literary genre) or to one of the ultimate components of reality (a Democritean atom or a Platonic form).[8]

Verbalization, argumentation, and the marshaling of facts and evidence are inextricably bound together in a process whose aim is the creation of ever better discourse; and progress can just as easily lie in a new figure of thought as in a new definition or proof, or a new scientific or mathematical discovery.[9] The besetting vices of the period are, accordingly, overingenuity, overcomplexity, and

143

technical ostentatiousness—not irresponsible rhetoric. A writer's message is far more likely to be submerged or subdivided into invisibility than it is to be projected more forcefully than it deserves through poetic and rhetorical overstatement, or to profit from the enthusiasm generated by the stylistic ornamentation that accompanies it. And when the speaker succeeds it is less through manipulation of his audience than through taking it into his confidence—allowing its members to share or even, if possible, to anticipate for themselves the excitement and exhilaration of discovery or pseudodiscovery. They become, to quote an unfriendly witness,

> most adept at letting themselves be taken in by new-fangled speech and at unwillingness to stick with what is already accepted and established, ever slaves to novelty and scorners of the conventional, wanting most of all—each of them—to be the speaker himself, and failing that, to compete with speakers at seeming quick in following the argument and to anticipate their telling points by applause—eager to perceive what is said before it is said and slow at perceiving its consequences; seeking to live in some other world . . . and so paying insufficient attention even to what is immediately at hand.

Thucydides (3.38.3–4) has Cleon speak these lines just before he characterizes the Athenian assembly as more like a crowd at a Sophistic epideixis than a deliberative body; and Cleon's picture of a situation in which speaker and audience alike are afflicted by a misplaced faith in discourse as a panacea forms an instructive contrast with his opponent Diodotus's attack on the opposite situation, in which distrust of discourse is so widespread that speakers must beware of sounding too informed and intelligent, or offering advice that seems too sensible (3.43.2–3). It is only the second situation that necessarily calls for a rhetorician and the various self-deprecatory ploys his art teaches. And self-deprecation does not become a characteristic mode of Greek eloquence until the fourth century.

The same holds true for the appeal to the emotions—another typical instance of rhetorical (and fourth-century) condescension. Among all the discourse components attested for the period, only the *Plaints* of Thrasymachus seem clearly oriented toward moving rather than informing an audience. If the surviving fragment on political strife is in fact from a companion piece devoted to allaying anger rather than arousing pity (see chapter 5), it suggests that the basis of the appeals the collection contained was much more intellectual than the title and Plato's summary description of its contents (*Phaedr.* 267c7–8) would indicate.

Skepticism about the attainability or communicability of knowledge, such as is maintained in Gorgias's treatise *On Not Being,* or relativism of the kind usually assumed to lie behind Protagoras's famous assertion that man is the measure of all things, might, if consistently maintained, have removed some of the inhibitions that operate in traditional societies to prevent full exploration of all of rhetoric's possibilities. If truth is unknowable, or incommunicable, or simply what seems so to a given observer at a given moment, a speaker can hardly be faulted for using an argument simply because it is persuasive—without being sure of the truth or falsity of the position it maintains.[10]

In practice, however, the very skepticism and relativism that made certain extreme uses of rhetoric conceivable would have tended to eliminate them as real possibilities. Protagoras's technique of "making the worse argument better" (80 B 6b) can only have involved—assuming a consistently relativistic understanding of "better" and "worse"—teaching a student to think, and make others think, about situations in ways that were better rather than worse for him. In Aristotle's example (*Rhet.* 2.24 1402a17–19) of how the system worked, the two arguments are the case for the rule and the case for the exception to the rule. The stronger man is likely, as a rule, to have been the aggressor in the fight whose origins form the subject of a *status coniecturalis* (see chapter 5). On the other hand, the exception can become the rule if one argues that the stronger man is unlikely, as a rule, to put himself in a situation where, as a rule, people like him turn out to have been the aggressors and are so suspected of having been at fault whether they were or not. In pleading his case the strong man will try to make the second argument apply rather than the first—the one that is "better" for him rather than the one that is worse. The imperialist will try to see—and make others see—his policy in terms of the position taken by the Athenians rather than the Corinthians in the *technē* that begins at Thucydides 1.68; and the democrat will do the same for the Periclean rather than the Alcibiadean account of the regime he favors (see chapter 6).[11] The method does not exclude in principle the attempt to find a better argument for every case, no matter how desperate or idiosyncratic; but this would only be feasible within the context of some Platonically conceived systematization of discourse, individual audience reaction, and the full range of possibilities open to each. Without such a systematization, a practical course of training would almost inevitably have to concentrate on those recurring questions that do, in the opinion of most people, have two sides, each one capable of being presented in both a better and a worse light.

When one turns from Protagoras to Gorgias and attempts to reconstruct a pedagogical program in the light of the latter's expressed doubts about the existence or communicability of knowledge, the gap between what is theoretically conceivable and what would have been practically possible or likely becomes even larger. The doubts found in the treatise *On Not Being* reappear in the *Helen,* where Gorgias reveals a very vivid sense of the state of ignorance and uncertainty that is habitual for the human psyche, the resulting tendency for the psyche to be guided by mere opinion, and the way virtually anything one sees or hears can cause the abandoning of one opinion for another. The powers that *logos* as a creator of opinion has are correspondingly immense: it can make the spectators at a tragedy weep as if the sufferings evoked by the dramatists' words were their own; it can use philosophical discourse to transform completely an audience's conception of the universe; it can overturn from one minute to the next in the course of debate the hearer's conception of what is valid and not valid; and it can charm and persuade a whole throng, even when untrue (*Helen* 8–14).

There is nothing, however, to suggest that, as some critics have maintained, Gorgias intended this analysis of the power of *logos* to be an indirect glorification of his own profession. His position is, to extrapolate on one of his own analogies, that of an experimenter in the use of mind-altering drugs testifying on behalf of someone (Helen) who has committed a crime under their influence. A fairly lengthy expatiation on the power of such drugs to make a person do things he or she would not do otherwise is perfectly appropriate in such a situation, but one would not expect a general eulogy of them, much less an attempt on the part of the speaker to impress on the audience the exceptional powers his own pharmacological expertise confers. If this is the thrust of Gorgias's rhetoric at this point, it is rhetoric of a fairly inept sort.

Moreover, even granting Gorgias a certain tactlessness, it is not at all certain that the situations he refers to are conceived as situations that the speaker manipulates to his own purpose.[12] Such manipulation is rather unlikely in one of the examples cited (philosophers discoursing on the nature of the universe were not normally thought of as skillful persuaders) and completely excluded in the case of another type of "victim" to the power of opinion mentioned later in the speech (16–17: the army as terrified by the sight of an enemy drawn up in battle array as it would be if the battle had already begun). Nor can it be said that the spectators at a tragedy are manipulated, since they are willing participants in the author's "deception." What army and audience perceive is the future suggested or the past reenacted (with perfect accuracy in many cases) in a fabric of sights and sounds that becomes as real as, or, in the case of tragedy, more real than life itself. There is no question here of an appeal to pathos that exaggerates the extent of a victim's suffering. Instead of an intentional widening of the gap between referent and meaning that is deliberately induced by the art of rhetorical suggestion, one has a narrowing of the gap between referent and signifier, or an inversion of their normal relationship. This narrowing can also come about through a process of manipulation, but on many occasions it is involuntary or self-induced: a particularly intense version of the eyewitness immediacy that had been seen from Homer on (see chapter 2) as a prime source of the power of poetry; or of the replacement of the real world by the world of discourse of which Cleon complains in his debate with Diodotus.

The role that *logos* may play in this process entitles it to be called a "wielder of power" (*dynastēs: Helen* 8), but not necessarily a technician (*dēmiourgos* [Socrates' word, not Gorgias's, at *Gorgias* 453a2]). Later writers can speak of rhetoric as a form of power (*dynamis*), or as possessing a *dynamis* of its own, but art and *dynamis* are distinct enough that at times (cf. Arist., *Rhet.* 1.2 1356a32–34; 1.4 1359b12–14; Quintilian 2.15.2) *dynamis* is explicitly contrasted with the exact knowledge (*epistēmē, scientia*) that regularly accompanies art. Nor in Gorgias's own discussion is there any general reference to *logos* as art to set against the possible implications of its general description as a *dynastēs*. Power, not artfulness, is the quality that makes it similar to those *technai* that operate by means of drugs (14) or "inspired verbal incantations" (10); and when a whole throng is charmed and persuaded (13) by a speech "professionally writ" (*technēi grapheis*), not "truthfully spoke" (*alētheiai lextheis*), the reference is to one very specific, not especially popular form that artful eloquence can take.[13] In what is almost certainly an echo of this passage, Socrates speaks of the "discourse-making" (*logopoios*) art as a subdivision (*morion*) of the art of incantations, the latter being the province of snake-charmers and the like, the former of crowd-charmers (Plato, *Euthydemus* 289e4–90a4); but this is probably yet another instance of later "rhetorization" of traditional material (see chapter 6).

In Gorgias himself, by contrast, the state of being persuaded does not have to be externally, or even self-, induced. It is more like the natural state of humankind—the result of a capacity for confusing illusion and reality that is, on the one hand, so basic that it hardly needs the skillful artificer of Socrates' definition to bring it into being and, on the other, so irrational that it might be expected to elude the power of such an artificer to control. And *logos* itself—more ability than art and more external force, perhaps, than indwelling ability—would be equally unlikely to be subject more than intermittently to the commands of an acquired set of techniques.

Further indication of the independence of power and art is provided by the fragment (B26) that speaks of "being" (*to einai*) as "lacking in visibility" (*aphanes*) when it does not coincide with (literally, "meet up with," "happen upon [*tychēi*]") seeming (*to do-*

kein)," and "seeming" as "lacking in power or strength" (*asthenes*) when it does not coincide with being. The language suggests that there is something casual and unpredictable about the way being and seeming "happen upon" each other (presumably, when the impression created by a speech is a true one); but it also suggests that the context Gorgias has in mind is an agonistic one. This context is explicit in A8, the Sophist's epitaph, composed for him by a kinsman:

> To train the soul to strive for virtue's prize
> none better arts than Gorgias did devise.

What suggests that setting in B26 as well is the term *asthenes*, for an agonistic context is the one in which the "strength" of an opinion would be most relevant, and in which coincidence with "being" would be most likely to be a source of strength. The average human soul is no match for the persuasiveness of *logos*; but a more equal contest can occur when *logos* is set against *logos*, and between two equally powerful *logoi* truth might well tip the scales. The possibility of such a coincidence between seeming and truth is not completely excluded, even by the skeptical arguments of the treatise *On Not Being*.[14]

The epitaph does not credit Gorgias with teaching virtue or excellence (*aretē*) itself, and he may well have disclaimed such ability (cf. Plato, *Meno* 95c). The art involved is much more limited, doing no more for men's souls than an athletic trainer would do for their bodies: equipping ability and ambition with the necessary competitive edge that would enable it to win the prize—or give as good an account of itself as possible—when pitted against that of other contestants in *aretē*. It would not be within Gorgias's province, any more than it would be in that of the athletic trainer, to supply an aspiring competitor with *aretē*—that is, ability—itself. What he can provide is, at most, incremental: pointers as to "what techniques will advance a man toward his goal if he is to win the most coveted glory that holy contests bring" (Pindar, *Olympian* 7.62–63). In the political and juridical contests Gorgias has in mind this would mean mastery of the best *logoi* possible or, in practical terms, the sample pieces that constituted Gorgias's *technē*.

(Cf., at Isocrates 15.183, the explicit comparison between the holds and positions [*schēmata*] taught to students of wrestling and the topoi [*ideai*] taught to the students of *logoi*.)

It would be in keeping with Gorgias's announced skepticism to assign a limited value to such pieces. They would be rather like torches and lanterns in a world where daylight does not exist. The alternative to the "appearance" they produce is total darkness—the situation in which being is *aphanes*—not, as it would be in Plato, the daylight of dialectic, for which the rhetorician's lamps and torches are an inadequate but occasionally necessary substitute. When, therefore, to use two possibly authentic examples attributed to Gorgias in Plato's dialogue, the rhetorician persuades a patient to avail himself of the services of a doctor (456b2–5) or a city to build a harbor (455d7–e2), he is not giving a layperson's explanation of medical or architectural technicalities—not shining his torch for the benefit of those who would be blinded if confronted with the daylight in which the specialist sees such matters. This is how the second example is interpreted—and "rhetoricized"—by later tradition (Cicero, *De or.* 1.62). But surely it would be more likely in such a situation—and more in keeping with Gorgias's view of man as a believing animal—for the specialist's credentials to be taken on faith, and the rhetor's services to be required elsewhere: in talking about the advantages of a new harbor for the overall economy and defense of the city, or the desirability of submitting to medical treatment, even though painful, if there is no other prospect of being restored to health. The speaker is casting his torchlight on areas with which the specialist is unaccustomed to dealing at all.

Both these examples are compatible with the assumption that when someone *is* accustomed to deal with an area he will know whereof he speaks. But even this degree of certainty may have been more than Gorgias was willing to acknowledge. Transposing Plato's famous cooking metaphor (*Gorgias* 462d7 ff.; see chapter 1) into Gorgianic terms, one might think of the speaker as a culinary specialist who takes a set of foods that are fairly tasteless—gustatorially *aphanes*—in their natural state, and subjects them to the various processes (aging, fermenting, diluting, purifying, concentrating, combining, cooking, and seasoning) necessary to make them distinguishable to the palate. The palate may be unable to pick out a preparation that highlights and renders perceptible the natural flavor from one that alters it by a sauce; but at the very least such preparation makes perceptible—if not identifiable—a flavor that otherwise would not be experienced at all. Whether the perceptions so produced in fact corresponded with reality in a given situation would obviously be a matter of some importance. But the insignificance of Gorgias's remarks on suitability to the occasion (*kairos*, discussed in chapter 5) suggests that it was a matter he regarded as beyond his power as trainer for contests in excellence to control—perhaps beyond anybody's power. The particular contest would have to determine how and whether the views a student selected to propound from some general *technē* coincided with "being," just as it would have the final say on the relative excellence of the contestants.

A trainer who cannot control the amount of excellence with which a competitor enters the contest, or the truth content of the *logoi* he chooses eventually to use, obviously cannot control the outcome. He can only do everything in his power to see that what there is of truth and excellence is not condemned to remain obscure, and trust that, if other trainers do the same, greater excellence and the greater strength of opinion when linked to being will make themselves felt in the long run. The attitude shows a naïveté not often encountered in rhetoricians, but it is typical of Gorgias as he is presented by Plato; and here, at any rate, Plato's testimony cannot be dismissed as simply another detail in a generally hostile portrayal of a Sophist. Once Polus has become truculent in defending his master against Socrates, Gorgias nevertheless insists that Socrates be given a full and fair hearing regardless of the consequences this may have for the way his own case fares in the contest that is in progress (463a4, d6–e4). Gorgias's pupil Proxenos, as described by Xenophon, showed the same sort of faith in the agonistic mechanism. He was consumed with a desire to excel which made him first pay money for Gorgias's instruction and then seek the widest possible field for the exercise of his talents by joining the expedition of the younger Cyrus. Yet he failed in the end to be a thoroughly effective commander because of his naïve tendency to believe that his own devotion to *aretē* was shared by everyone (*Anabasis* 2.6.16–20).

It is doubtful that this naïveté extended, as Plato would have us believe, to a complacent exaltation of his own uninformed presentation of a theme over the informed one of an expert (*Gorgias* 452e1–8, 456c2–6, 459c3–5), for Gorgianic discourse operates perforce in situations where expertise as Plato understands it is not available. Socratic teleology, however, demanded an ultimate goal for the display of competitive excellence for which Gorgias trained his students and which he, like most of his contemporaries, regarded as an end in itself. And once Plato had decided that the goal was "persuasion"—the implanting of opinions in an audience—it was easy to assume that, in the absence of stated objective criteria for determining the character of these opinions, Gorgias must have operated with subjective ones instead: acceptability to an audience and general agreeability, whether based on pleasure or the appearance of truth.

There is nothing, however, in either the surviving fragments or in other authors' accounts of Gorgias, to confirm this assumption. To accept the isolated testimony of Plato at this point is to read the presuppositions and methods of later rhetoric into a characteristically fifth-century phenomenon. Gorgias's skepticism, like Protagoras's relativism, obviously shared the rhetorician's recognition of the problematic character of human communication. But having recognized the problem, both men chose, by and large, to circumvent it rather than seek a solution along rhetorical lines. Their main activity appears to have been directed toward the study and presentation of those arguments, themes, and techniques whose occurrence was sufficiently widespread that their overall usefulness was independent of the changing tastes of audiences, or the changing availability and communicability of truth in various circumstances. To proceed further than this toward the production of a genuine art of rhetoric would have required precisely those intellectual disciplines of which there is no trace elsewhere in Protagoras, Gorgias, or any of their contemporaries: a systematic psychology that would countenance the possibility of constructing a particular piece of persuasion according to preset plan and an epistemology that would make possible the idea of an unmediated verbal rendering of reality by reference to which rhetorical deviations can be identified, characterized, and put to conscious use.

A morphology of the real developed on the basis of such a psychology and epistemology is more or less taken for granted in the *Phaedrus,* concerned as that dialogue is to lay down the conditions a true art of rhetoric must satisfy rather than to decide whether there were practical steps that would make satisfying these conditions possible, and—if so—what these steps were. The practical steps were left for Aristotle—or perhaps he was beginning to take them at the same time Plato was writing the *Phaedrus.* Whatever the exact chronology, traces of the order in which they were taken may still be detectable in the version of his work on rhetoric that survives. If the *Phaedrus* is the most striking testimony to the breadth of the gap separating rhetoric from its antecedents, the *Rhetoric* testifies in an equally striking way to the labor required to bridge it.[15] Aristotle organizes his discussion of rhetorical argumentation, in a way that has always created problems of interpretation, along two rather different lines. One of these involves a set of "premises" (*protaseis*) called "specific" (*idiai*) in that their validity is confined to a single type of subject matter: moral values, political policy, human emotions, criminal psychology, etc.; the other involves a set of *topoi* ("modes of argumentation") called general (*koinoi*) in that they can be applied to any subject whatsoever. The principle of classification is not entirely clear. It is possible, on the one hand, to think of *protaseis* that are perfectly general: "The whole is greater than any of its parts," for example, by contrast with "A straight line is the shortest distance between two points," which applies only to the geometry of plane surfaces. On the other hand, if one grants that predicability of opposites by opposites ("If friends are deserving of love, then enemies are deserving of hate") is a general *topos* (the first one listed in the enumeration of *Rhet.* 2.23), why not make "cui bono" or "cherchez la femme" a specific *topos* confined to the realm of criminology?

The exact relationship between the two schemes is not likely to be determined, for it is something Aristotle himself may never have worked out completely. But it is possible to say something about the wider affinities of each method within the context of Aristotelian logic and rhetoric.[16] The series of special *protaseis* whose listing accounts for over a third of the whole treatise is, as many scholars have pointed out, intimately linked to Aristotle's doctrine of the syllogism. In effect, the *protaseis* are a series of premises designed to facilitate, in as many situations as possible, the discovery of the appropriate middle term that is vital for the application of syllogistic reasoning to a problem. The natural scientist, confronted with the task of finding a possible proof for the sphericity of the moon, casts around for a class of things to which the moon belongs and which is itself a subdivision within the class of spherical bodies. He may find its identifying property to be that of casting a round shadow, thus permitting the construction of the syllogism:

Bodies that always cast round shadows are spherical.
The moon is a body that always casts a round shadow.
The moon is spherical.

Similar procedures will work for the just or the advantageous or the possible or likely or whatever is assumed to be, in a given type of discussion, the ultimate standard of reference by which any proposal or contention is going to be judged. By providing a list of things of which these categories can be predicated Aristotle allows the items on the list to serve as middle terms in syllogisms that place the object of a speaker's particular contention in the desired larger category. The method works on the most trivial level as well as the most significant. Thus the sort of syllogism to which *Rhet.* 1.12 1373a31–32 points would be the following:

Objects easily carried away and hidden in small places [*ta eu bastakta kai en mikrois topois aphanizomena*] are likely to be stolen.
The ring found on the person of the accused is an object easily carried away and hidden in small places.
The ring on the person of the accused is likely to have been stolen.

The *topoi* of the *Rhetoric* are less a general complement to such specific *protaseis* than an alternative to them and the syllogistic reasoning they presuppose. Though the argumentational modes involved are more varied than the syllogism, some of them could be reduced to syllogistic form.[17] Conversely, the syllogism itself could be recast as a *topos,* its "primary" mode becoming the *topos* "from predicates predicated of predicates" (*ex hyparchontōn hyparchousin*) or the like. Certain items, moreover, appear under both rubrics in Aristotle's treatment. The whole system of *protasis* reasoning, for example, insofar as it involves a listing of the sort of thing men consider desirable or undesirable, is presented in 2.23 1399b32–1400a4 as the single *topos* devoted to a consideration of *telika kephalaia* (see chapter 5): usefulness, feasibility, ease of attainment, advantageousness to self or harmfulness to one's enemies, or whatever other qualities lead men to embark on a contemplated course of action. Induction (1398a33–98b20) is a single *topos* among the twenty-eight listed in 2.23. Elsewhere, however, induction is represented by its rhetorical "counterpart," example (1.2 1356a35–57b36); and example and enthymeme (the rhetorical counterpart to the syllogism) are said to constitute the entirety of rhetorical argumentation. Amplification is mentioned in 2.18 1391b30–92a1 as a general topic, to be treated apart from the specific subjects with which *protaseis* are connected; yet when the treatment comes (2.19 1393a9–19), such general discussion is said to be pointless; and the reader is referred back to the specific *protaseis* on the good and the various degrees of greater and less of which it is susceptible (1.6–7).

In all instances of fluctuation in classification, it is the *protasis* rubric that contains the more extensive discussion, which suggests that the *topos* treatment was either less important in Aristotle's total scheme, or had come to be so by the time he completed the version of his teaching that has come down to us. The latter view is supported by the close links that connect, on the one hand, the *protaseis* of the *Rhetoric* with the sections of the *Prior Analytics* where the doctrine of the syllogism is set forth,[18] and on the other hand, the *topos* sections of the *Rhetoric* with the *Topica* (followed in the ancient collections of the philosopher's treatises by a discussion of fallacies, the *Sophistikōn elenchōn*, just as the *topos* chapter in the *Rhetoric* is immediately followed by one devoted to pieces of reasoning that appear to be valid but are not [*phainomena enthymēmata*]). The *Topica* is generally thought to represent an earlier phase in the development of Aristotle's logic than the *Prior Analytics*.[19] Moreover, it is in the *topoi* chapter that references to the argumentative procedures used by Aristotle's predecessors are concentrated: the *technai* of Corax, Theodorus, Callippus, and Pamphilus, all of which are said to have consisted of one or more of the *topoi* in the process of being enumerated (see chapter 5).

The same chronological sequence is suggested by the fact that *ēthos* and *pathos* are given an exclusively "protasistic" treatment, in the form of a series of premises having to do with the usual causes and objects of various passions, the sort of persons subject to them, and the character traits exhibited by certain classes of people (young and old, rich and poor). A widely held and probably correct view of the composition of the *Rhetoric* makes both *ēthos* and *pathos* later inclusions in a project that originally conceived of rhetoric, not as a combination of dialectic with other subjects such as politics and psychology, but simply as a "counterpart" to dialectic, sharing with dialectic both the generality of its subject matter (presentable, therefore, exclusively in terms of *topoi*) and its restriction to logical, or apparently logical, means of persuasion.[20] The whole shift in the focus of the treatise—if the prevailing view of the existence and character of the shift is correct—is away from organization according to components or modes of discourse and in the direction of organization exclusively according to subject matter: the various areas, each of them studied in depth by its own discipline such as ethics or politics, to which the specific *protaseis* that the rhetorician must master belong. The gaps in what is known about these areas are assumed to be sufficiently small that there is no longer any need for the virtuoso, but often fallacious, leaps practiced by *topos* logic: from the desirability of loving friends, for example, to that of hating enemies, or from a man's proved willingness to commit a crime for small gain to—*a fortiori*—his presumed willingness to do so for large gain; or from one extreme term to the other in almost any piece of "proportional" or analogical reasoning (present among the *topoi* of 2.23 [1399a35–b4], yet ultimately slated, one suspects, for demotion to the purely stylistic role of supplying a basis for metaphors [cf. 3.4 1407a15–16, 3.6 1408a8–9]). Everything can be accomplished in securer fashion by a chain of syllogisms relating particulars to well-defined classes and these classes in turn to other ones, whether contained, containing, or overlapping.

The close relationship between Aristotle's doctrine of the syllogism and the dialectic of collection and division on which the rhetoric and rhetorical analyses of the *Phaedrus* rest has been pointed out by historians of logic.[21] Here, as elsewhere, the *Phaedrus* seems to record the point of arrival, whereas the *Rhetoric* records certain individual stages along the way as well. The point of arrival is the same in both cases, however, and it is the logical end point of the overall fourth-century evolution toward a radical separation of content from form. Aristotle's characteristic reclassification of the whole realm of rhetoric according to the nature of the things dealt with and their location within the realm of time (future advantage and disadvantage, past right and wrong, present [or timeless] noble and base) rather than, say, the mode of discourse involved (hortatory, constative, evaluative) is merely the most famous—and influential—of the transformations involved.[22]

The breadth and persistence of such influence would have been impossible, of course, without the conviction, originating with the philosophers of the Socratic tradition but gradually penetrating to all areas of educated discourse, as training in philosophy spread and a *koinē* of philosophical belief developed, that the geography of the real had been definitively mapped out in its main outlines. And that conviction was also, in its initial stages, an essential prerequisite for the expansion and transformation of fifth-century *technē* into rhetoric—just as essential, in this respect, as the creation of a written discourse that could make the same sort of total claims on an audience's attention that spoken discourse does. The decisive steps in both areas were taken in Plato's generation and, in significant part, through the activity of Plato himself: the "saving" of the individual phenomena as reflections, imitations, or approximations of an unchanging order of reality, and the saving of the power, color, and effectiveness of individual pieces of oral discourse as embodiments, captured in writing, of permanently valid messages perfectly adjusted to the needs of unique situations. Both achievements, however arrived at, were necessary conditions for a flourishing art of rhetoric. Coming, as they did, not separately in time, or in different authors, the two achievements may well have been something of greater importance still: a more than sufficient condition for the unchallenged dominance the rhetorical conception of artistic discourse was to enjoy for the next two thousand years.

Notes

Chapter 1 Rhetoric, Neorhetoric, Protorhetoric

1. The word *rhētōr* is used originally for any able political or courtroom speaker (see W. Pilz, *Der Rhetor im attischen Staat* [Leipzig, 1934], 7–28); but professionalism in these areas was always regarded with a certain amount of suspicion. (The meaning "rhetorician," "teacher of eloquence," is not attested until the Hellenistic period.)

2. Aeschines uses the adjective *rhētorikos* (3.163) and the adverb *rhētorikōs* (1.71), but only to mean "pertaining to a speaker" or "eloquently."

3. Against the general tendency to make Socrates a protestor against the "degrading, disgusting and unworthy" character of Lysias's speech, see M. Nussbaum, "Poetry, Goodness, and Understanding in Plato's *Phaedrus*," in J. Moravcsik and P. Tempko, eds., *Plato on Beauty, Wisdom and the Arts* (Totowa, N.J., 1982), 81–82.

4. See the discussion in Arist., *Rhet.* 3.15, and Anaximenes (?), *Rhet. ad. Alex.* 29 61.11–64.23 Fuhrmann.

5. The *ad hominem* elements in Socrates' presentation have been largely ignored by commentators on the *Phaedrus*. See, however, R. Brumbaugh, *Plato for the Modern Age* (New York, 1962), 105, and E. Asmis, "Psychagogia in Plato's Phaedrus," *Illinois Studies* 11 (1986): 161–65.

6. On the contrast between Platonic and Aristotelian dialectic see, in general, F. Solmsen, "Dialectic without the Forms," in G. E. L. Owen, ed., *Aristotle on Dialectic: Third Symposium Aristotelicum* (Oxford, 1970), 49–68 = *Kleine Schriften* 3 (Hildesheim, 1982), 279–98.

7. The three possible ways of using premises are never enumerated in this fashion by Aristotle himself, but some such reconstruction is necessary to explain how the catalogue of premises offered in Book 2 can be relevant to both *ēthos-* and *pathos-*based arguments.
8. See D. A. Russell, *Criticism in Antiquity* (Berkeley and Los Angeles, 1981), 115–16.
9. See A. Scaglione, *The Classical Theory of Composition* (Chapel Hill, N.C., 1972), 74 ff. The idea of "normal" word order is an essential part of ancient discussions of the subject, even if they "defined it neither too categorically nor quite clearly" (p. 88).
10. See the translation and discussion in Russell, *Criticism in Antiquity,* 176–78.
11. R. Genette, *Figures of Literary Discourse* (Engl. tr., New York, 1982), 47–48.
12. Cf., for example, I. Düring, *Aristoteles* (Heidelberg, 1966), 126. The general *letteraturizzazione* of rhetorical procedures into other genres is discussed by G. Kennedy, *Classical Rhetoric and Its Christian and Secular Tradition from Ancient to Modern Times* (Chapel Hill, N.C., 1980), 108 ff.
13. Aristotle's contemporary, the author (Anaximenes?) of the *Rhetorica ad Alexandrum,* sees the orator's appeal to probability as involving, in similar fashion, those things of which "models" (*paradeigmata*) already exist in the minds of the hearers. The speaker's picture of himself and others will be accepted only to the extent that it consists of familiar patterns of character and behavior (7 30.27–31.4 Fuhrmann).
14. Notably Horace in the *Ars poetica* and Plutarch in *On How Poets Should be Read.* Cf. Russell, *Criticism in Antiquity,* 93–95.
15. *Heuresis* and *diathesis* (arrangement) are already contrasted in Plato's *Phaedrus* 236a, but not as part of an exhaustive, systematic set of categories.
16. Cf. R. M. Weaver's view of rhetoric's proper goal: to "combine action and understanding into a whole that is greater than scientific perception" (*The Ethics of Rhetoric* [Chicago, 1953], 24–25).
17. Wayne Booth's *The Rhetoric of Fiction,* 2d ed. (Chicago, 1983), and *The Rhetoric of Irony* (Chicago, 1974), are conspicuous examples.
18. Even E. D. Hirsch, Jr., a self-proclaimed reactionary on the contemporary critical scene, regards the study of style in literature as "a study of the *fusion* of form with content." It is only the craft of "learning" (or teaching) "how to write" that legitimately "assumes the separation of form and content" (*The Philosophy of Composition* [Chicago, 1977], 141).

19. See, for a comprehensive survey and critique, P. Ricoeur, *The Rule of Metaphor* (Engl. tr. [Toronto, 1977] of *La Métaphore vive* [1975]). I. A. Richard's redefinition of rhetoric as "a study of misunderstanding and its remedies" (*The Philosophy of Rhetoric* [New York, 1936], 3) involves a similar inversion—in which plain, unambiguous transmission of meaning is regarded as a goal, rather than as an essential given, for the whole discipline.

20. Ricoeur, *The Rule of Metaphor*, 131. The citation in the text restores an italics omitted by the translator ("*except one*") and corrects one misprint ("unsuitable" for "suitable" in "none of the acceptations . . . is suitable" ["aucune des acceptances . . . ne convient"]).

21. See, for example, W. J. Bate, *From Classic to Romantic* (Cambridge, Mass., 1946), and M. H. Abrams, *The Mirror and the Lamp* (New York, 1953).

22. Cicero, *De Or.* 1.90: "ita nati . . . ut et blandire . . . possemus et rem gestam exponere et id quod intenderemus confirmare et quod contra diceretur refellere, ad extremum deprecari et conqueri, quibus in rebus omnis oratorum versaretur facultas."

23. See H. Cherniss, *Aristotle's Criticism of Presocratic Philosophy* (Baltimore, 1935), 219 ff.

24. The analogy between different languages (or dialects) and different manners of presentation is explicit in Plato's *Apology* 17d–18a (Socrates likened to a foreigner [*xenos*] presenting his case in a language [*phōnē*] and manner [*tropos*] to which the jury is not accustomed).

25. Cf. Plato, *Pol.* 304cd, where rhetoric's proper task (assigned to it by the art of the statesman) is persuasion through "mythological parable and example" (*mythologia*) rather than "[philosophical, rational] instruction" (*didachē*), and *Laws* 4.723c8–d4, on the obligation—incumbent on lawgiver as well as lyric poet or rhetor—to supply the substantive message of his texts with a persuasive proem.

Chapter 2 Oral Poetry and Oral Eloquence

1. For an attempt to explain the use of the term *hypothesis* by reference to Aristotelian and post-Aristotelian notions of the nature of a fictional or mimetic plot, see W. Trimpi, "The Ancient Hypotheses of Fiction: An Essay in the Origins of Literary Theory," *Traditio* 27 (1971): 1–78. But the attempt requires stretching the meaning of the Greek word beyond all plausible limits.

2. Pre-Platonic references to artistic imitation are concerned primarily with the reproducing of external appearances, utterances, and move-

ments—art as mimicry rather than mimesis. See G. F. Else, "Imitation in the Fifth Century," *Classical Philology* 53 (1958): 73–90.

3. On being asked why he never "deceived" the Thessalians, Simonides is said to have replied that they were not sufficiently intelligent (Plutarch, *De aud. poet.* 15c)—perhaps an anticipation of Gorgias's attitude (unless, as Wilamowitz suggested [*Sappho und Simonides* (Berlin, 1913), 143], the anecdote belongs in fact to Gorgias rather than Simonides). The difference between such "deception" and characteristically rhetorical ways of misleading an audience is further discussed in chapter 8.

4. See A. B. Lord, *The Singer of Tales* (Cambridge, Mass., 1960), 27–28.

5. It makes no difference for our present purposes whether the text was Cynaithos's own, falsely ascribed by him to Homer, or—as others believe—an earlier text that Cynaithos claimed to have composed himself.

6. Homer's likening of Odysseus's narrative skill to that of a poet (*Odyssey* 17.513–21) and the similarity between Hesiod, *Theogony* 27, and *Odyssey* 19.203 (the ability of, respectively, the Muses and Odysseus to tell lies like truth) do not seem to me to justify the picture offered by some scholars of Homer as a poet concerned with "the inevitable difference between actual experiences and their retelling in song" (S. Murnaghan, *Disguise and Recognition in the Odyssey* [Princeton, N.J., 1987], 167). Cf., in addition, W. G. Thalmann, *Conventions of Form and Thought in Early Greek Poetry* (Baltimore, 1984), 170 ff.

7. See K. von Fritz, "ΝΟΟΣ and NOEIN in the Homeric Poems," *Classical Philology* 38 (1943): 79–93.

8. See also E. A. Havelock, *The Muse Learns to Write* (New Haven, Conn., 1986). The rest of Havelock's work subsequent to *Preface to Plato* (Oxford, 1963) is collected or cited in *The Literate Revolution in Greece and Its Cultural Consequences* (Princeton, N.J., 1982). W. J. Ong, *Orality and Literacy* (London, 1982) is perhaps the best general introduction to the problem, extensively indebted to Havelock in dealing with antiquity, but supplemented by much valuable material from postclassical and non-Western sources.

9. Translated as *Of Grammatology* (Baltimore, 1976). For discussions of Derrida's work and influence, see J. N. Culler, *On Deconstruction* (Ithaca, N.Y., 1982), 85–226.

10. The deeper implication of both views—for our understanding of the development of the Western philosophical consciousnesses (Havelock) or of the nature of meaning in a work of literature (Derrida)—are, inevitably, beyond the scope of the present book, concerned as it is with rhetoric in its narrow, classical sense.

Chapter 3 Tact and Etiquette

1. *The I-Li or Book of Etiquette and Ceremonial* (Engl. tr., London, 1917), 1:xiii (quoted in R. T. Oliver, *Communication and Culture in Ancient India and China* [Syracuse, 1971], 150).

2. See, in addition to the work of Oliver, *Communication,* M. Bloch, ed., *Political Language and Oratory in Traditional Society* (New York, 1975). Oliver notes that "in all the vast accumulation of Asian writing there is virtually no work whatever that is explicitly devoted to rhetoric" (*Communication,* 260). He believes that "implicit" attention to rhetoric is ubiquitous in China and India, "as an essential and integral part of generalized philosophical speculation" (p. 260). But this belongs properly to the "aggrandized" notion of the discipline held by some of the neorhetoricians referred to in chapter 1. The solitary exception, among authors Oliver discusses, is the Chinese prince Han Fei-Tzu, whose Machiavellian theories of persuasion are summarized on pp. 216–33.

3. As West notes in his commentary on Hesiod, *Works and Days,* 202–12.

4. The term *ainos* does not apply, of course, to narratives of past situations that are similar, and so relevant, to present ones (Phoenix's story of Meleager in *Iliad* 9.524–605, for example), or to extended personifications such as Phoenix's account of Disaster (*Atē*) and Supplications (*Litai*) in *Iliad* 9.502–12; Hesiod's picture of Justice spurned and turning on her persecutors (*Works and Days* 217–24); or Pindar's laudatory passages on "Quietude" (*Pythian* 8.1–12) and "Lawfulness" and her sisters (*Olympian* 13.6–10). Nor are the examples and personifications in such passages rhetorical in the way an *ainos* is. Personification is probably the simplest and most natural way of talking about juridical and sociopolitical phenomena that the archaic Greek language would find it difficult to handle directly. Like Phoenix's use of Meleager as an example, Hesiod's attempt to deal with the concept of legal and social retribution through the "personification" *Dikē* would be rhetorical in an Aristotelian context, in which example is understood as the rhetorical alternative to dialectical induction, and in which there exists a philosophical vocabulary that allows one to speak of retribution. Neither is rhetorical in early epic, where the alternative formulations are not readily available.

5. Chinese rhetoric knows a similar though more obvious form of remonstrance, in which a prince is made to consent to the moral of a fable before discovering that he is its real subject. Examples are found frequently, as my friend and student Han Sessie informs me, in the Confucian *Tso Chuan* and *Shih Chi.*

6. The most recent—and best—discussion is in G. W. Most, *The Measures of Praise* (Göttingen, 1985), 133–213. But many obscurities remain.

7. Cf., for Pindar's appeals to the hearer's exceptional judgment and taste, *Olympian* 2.82 ff., 11.10; *Pythian* 2.72 ff., 3.80 ff.; *Nemean* 7.12–19.

8. More precisely, since the publication of E. L. Bundy's influential *Studia Pindarica* (Berkeley, 1962).

9. The risk is even greater when one passes from Pindar himself to infer such an "ideology of exclusiveness" for archaic praise poetry in general. See, for example, the discussion in G. Nagy, *The Best of the Achaeans* (Baltimore, 1979), 239–41. What is true of the Pindaric epinician is almost certainly not true of epic and gnomic *laudatio*.

10. For the term "figured speech," see Demetrius, *On Style* 287–89, with the discussion in F. Ahl, "The Art of Safe Criticism," *American Journal of Philology* 105 (1984): 176 ff. Intimations and innuendos are perhaps to be found in Alcaeus's famous series of Ship of State allegories (see, most recently, the thorough discussion in B. Gentili, *Poetry and Its Public in Ancient Greece* [Engl. tr., Baltimore, 1988], 197–215). It is equally possible, however, that, as Gentili suggests, allegory there had the purely practical arhetorical function of providing the members of Alcaeus's faction with a private language for use among themselves; and the fables of Archilochus could have been a similar series of *poèmes à clef.*

11. There is thus a striking parallel between the subdivisions of epideictic eloquence recognized by the late writer Menander Rhetor and the subdivisions of lyric poetry recognized by Alexandrian editors of Pindar and his contemporaries and predecessors. Lament, encomium, funeral eulogy, marriage celebration, and victory congratulation all figure prominently on both lists. I am skeptical, however, of the more far-reaching similarities between epideictic and lyric that some scholars detect—those, for example, adduced by Francis Cairns throughout his *Generic Composition in Greek and Latin Literature* (Edinburgh, 1972) to show that the rules of arrangement found in Menander reflect canons of composition extending back to the archaic age.

Chapter 4 Allegory and Rhetoric

1. The interpretation is reported and attributed to Theagenes of Rhegium (= FVS 8 A 2) in the B Scholia to *Iliad* 21.67.

2. See the stimulating discussion in G. M. Most, "Rhetorik und Hermeneutik: Zur Konstitution der Neuzeitlichkeit," *Antike und Abendland* 30 (1984): 62–79.

3. Aristotelian examples, characteristically, fall between the two categories: rather more allegorical than rhetorical at *Politics* 8.6.1341b2–8 (Athena's casting away of the flute she invented is a poetic way of saying that flute playing does not contribute to the development of the rational faculties), and rather more rhetorical than allegorical at 2.9 1269b27–31 (Homer's story of Ares and Aphrodite is a commentary on the tendency of soldiers to be, or to fancy themselves, great lovers).

4. On rhetorical overcoding, see U. Eco, *A Theory of Semiotics* (Bloomington, Ind., 1976), 278–79.

5. The question of priority is as difficult to answer in dealing with Antisthenes and Plato as it is with Isocrates and Plato (see chapter 7).

6. See, in general, J. Pepin, *Mythe et allégorie* (Aubier, 1958), 97–99; and, for Theagenes' successors in the fifth century, N. J. Richardson, "Homeric Professors in the Age of the Sophists," *PCPS* 21 (1975): 65–81.

7. The highly wrought, idiosyncratic style of Heraclitus may well result, in part, from a self-conscious attempt to give his doctrines the attention-attracting power that attaches to the new and strange, and the respect that attaches to oracular opaqueness. But it is difficult to determine the character—or existence—of such pre-Parmenidean rhetoric without a clearer idea than we now have of the role the surviving material was intended to play in the overall presentation and dissemination of Heraclitean doctrine. See, for three strikingly divergent reconstructions, the articles of J. E. Barnes, C. H. Kahn, and Kevin Robb in Kevin Robb, ed., *Language and Thought in Early Greek Philosophy* (La Salle, Ill., 1983), 91–107, 110–24, and 182–201.

8. The reverse process, prose paraphrase of a piece of verse, was to become a standard rhetorical exercise (cf. Quintilian 1.9.1 and 10.5.4–8; Theon, 2.62.10 ff. and 2.65.23 Spengel; Dio of Prusa 18.19). Either or both processes may have been involved in the work of another Socratic, Critias, whose *Polity of the Spartans* seems to have existed in both a prose and a poetic version (cf. the parallel accounts of drinking customs in 88B6 and 33). Significantly, however, there are no other "pre-Socratic" instances of this particular testimony to a belief in the independence of content and literary medium.

9. See, for example, E. A. Havelock, *The Liberal Temper in Greek Politics* (New Haven, Conn., 1957), 91–94 and 408–9.

10. The relevant parallels are as follows: (1) Herodotus 3.108–9 = Plato, *Prot.* 320d–21b (the survival of various animal species attributed to a kind of compensatory distribution that provides each one with a characteristic advantage in the struggle for existence); (2) Euripides, *Suppliants* 913–15 = *Prot.* 328a (the process of social conditioning, by which everyone "learns" right and reverence [Protagoras] or "excel-

lence" [Euripides], compared to learning a language); (3) *On Ancient Medicine* 4–5 = *Prot.* 322cd, 324d–25b, and 327cd (the notion of a skill necessary for survival—right and reverence in the one case, the ability to distinguish beneficial food from harmful in the other—which fails to be recognized for what it is because everyone possesses it: no one can afford to be a nonprofessional [*idiōtēs*] in such an area); and (4) Sophocles, *Antigone* 370–75 = *Prot.* 322d (a review of human civilization in its technological, linguistic, and sociopolitical aspects concluded by a reference to the outcast condition ["cityless" in Sophocles, a "disease of the city" in the *Protagoras*] of the man who cannot accommodate himself to civilization's ways).

11. Cf. E. R. Dodds, *The Ancient Concept of Progress* (Oxford, 1973), 6.

12. Cf. Aristophanes, *Frogs* 440–43, 1152–69, 1178, 1265 (Aeschylean long-windedness), 945, 962–63 (Euripidean logic), 945, 1139–43 (Aeschylean obscurity and Euripidean clarity), 948, 1181, 1192 (Aeschylean distortion and Euripidean accuracy), 959–63 (Aeschylean preposterousness and Euripidean relevance).

13. Cf., for example, Strabo 1.2.8.

14. On the Sophistic affinities of the criticism, see M. Carroll, *Aristotle's Poetics XXV in the Light of Homeric Scholarship* (Baltimore, 1889), 10–12.

15. E. A. Havelock, "The Oral Composition of Greek Drama," *Quaderni Urbinati* 35 (1980): 93–99, rightly stresses the play's "didactic" content, but "rhetoricizes" unduly, I think, by dwelling on its indirect aspects: the "grandiose and heroic" setting which has the effect of "making the message the more effective by distancing it from the present" (p. 99). In view of the violence of the reaction (Herodotus 6.21) to the contemporary subject matter of Phrynichos's *Sack of Miletus*, performed twenty-five years earlier at Athens, it is unlikely that a different "setting" for Aeschylus's theme would have been any less effective.

16. On *orthoepeia* (FVS 80 B 26) see, in general, C.-J. Classen, "The Study of Language amongst Socrates' Contemporaries," in *Sophistik* (Darmstadt, 1976), 223–26. Surviving reports from early (fourth-century) sources suggest that Protagoras was concerned with both linguistic consistency and referential accuracy. Among the topics discussed were the maintenance of "logical" or "natural" genders, each linked to corresponding morphological formations (B III 6–8); accuracy and consistency in the differentiation of verbal moods (B III 6–8—cf. the criticism of *Iliad* 1.1); and, possibly, similar care with regard to tense (B III 24). Concern for maintaining the proper as against the figurative use of words (*kyriologia*) is also possible, but the evidence here is

confined to the late testimony of Hermias (B III 5). See R. Pfeiffer, *History of Classical Scholarship* (Oxford, 1968), 37–39.

17. See, for Euripides, W. Ludwig, *Sapheneia* (Diss. Bonn, 1957).

18. The metaphor at 1431–32, "Do not raise up a lion cub in your city, but if you do, see that you humor it in its ways," is a transparently obvious, if effective, reference to Alcibiades. Contrast the "prerhetorical" use of the same image in Aeschylus's famous stanzas (*Agamemnon* 717–36) on the dangers of rearing lion cubs. There the easy translatability of figurative into "ordinary" discourse which rhetorical theory posits is conspicuously absent: is the lion's whelp Paris? or Helen? or any and/or all of the ultimately disastrous illusions which people are and have been in the habit of cultivating?

Chapter 5 Technē *and Text*

1. The passages quoted are from, respectively, R. C. Jebb, *The Greek Orators from Antiphon to Isaeus* (Cambridge, 1886), 1:cxxvii, and J. D. Denniston, *Greek Prose Style* (Oxford, 1953), 12.

2. See B. Gentili and G. Cerri, *Le teorie del discorso storico nel pensiero greco e la storiografia romana arcaica* (Rome, 1975), 22–26.

3. "Gorgias . . . in the Helena has furnished causal explanations . . . that could be applied, so far as I can see, to *any misdeed whatever*." A. W. H. Adkins, "Form and Content in Gorgias's *Helen* and *Palamedes*: Rhetoric, Philosophy, Inconsistency and Invalid Argument in Some Greek Thinkers," in J. P. Anton and Anthony Preus, eds., *Essays in Ancient Philosophy* (Albany, N.Y., 1983), 2:122. It need not follow, however, as Adkins maintains (2:117), that Gorgias is simply "manipulating language . . . to prove a case ad hoc."

4. There is no reason to believe that the Funeral Oration was ever much longer than it is now. The references to Xerxes as the "Persian Zeus" and to vultures as the "living tombs" of the bodies they have consumed usually assigned to the *Epitaphios* (82B5a) may even go back, like similar citations from the speeches of Pericles, to memories of an oral performance. They certainly show a boldness in the use of metaphor that has no parallel in the text that survives.

5. B12; cf. his reproach to the "unladylike" nightingale (Philomela) for covering him with her droppings (B23).

6. Timaeus is usually assumed to be the source of Diodorus's famous account (12.53.1 ff. = 82 A 4) of the impression these devices made when the Athenians first encountered them during Gorgias's visit in 427 B.C. Cicero's attribution of them to Gorgias (*Or.* 175–76) may go back to Aristotle, but all that appears in Aristotle himself is, first, the

discussion of antithesis, rhyme, and parallelism in *Rhet.* 3.9, where Gorgias is not mentioned and the examples are mostly Isocratean; and, second, a general statement (*Rhet.* 3.1 1404a24 = 82A29) about the poetic coloring of Gorgias's style.

7. The style of the speech of Agathon in Plato's *Symposium* (195a–97e) which reminds Socrates of Gorgias is recognizably that of the demonstration texts, but there is no trace of that style in the places where it might be expected in the *Gorgias*.

8. *Prytaneion* is, of course, Plato's expression (*Prot.* 337d); but similar characterizations appear in Thucydides (2.38.1–39.1 and 2.41.1) and Isocrates (15.298–306). They were doubtless commonplaces of Attic panegyric in the late fifth century.

9. For the argument that "literacy in the Ionian cities and islands had a head start over the mainland," see E. A. Havelock, *The Literate Revolution in Greece and Its Cultural Consequences* (Princeton, N.J., 1982), 21–22. The evidence is partly literary (Ionic is the original dialect for all books composed in prose), partly epigraphical (the presence of cursive letter styles in sixth-century Ionian inscriptions—presumably developed to facilitate writing on papyrus rolls and so an indication of their increasing use and importance).

10. The significance of the difference between the two types of work was first pointed out, to my knowledge, by George Kennedy, "The Earliest Rhetorical Handbooks," *American Journal of Philology* 80 (1959): 169 ff.

11. See Radermacher's commentary on B XXIII 13 and 15 and B XXIV 14 and 16, with the earlier discussions cited there and, for Isocrates, K. Barwick, "Das Problem der isokrateischen Techne," *Philologus* 107 (1963): 42–60. Radermacher's contention that the works referred to cannot be rhetorical treatises is certainly correct, but they are probably less frequently, as he suggests, "orationes ad regulam expolitae" than "orationes regulae vice fungentes." *Ad regulam expolitio* presupposes the prior existence of a body of rules, and of this there is little clear trace during the period with which we are now concerned. Whatever the total proportion of precept to example was, there are no grounds for the view that "when the ancient sources speak of *technē* or *ars* they always mean theoretical instruction and usually a written exposition or handbook, never collections of commonplaces" (Kennedy, 54–55).

12. Recognized as a general possibility by A. Lesky, *Geschichte der griechischen Literatur* (Bern, 1963), 387, this view is maintained, for Gorgias, by H.-A. Koch, *Homo mensura* (Diss. Lübeck), 71, and, for Anaxagoras, by E. A. Havelock. See Havelock's suggestion (*Literate Revolution,* 322) as to the nature of the *biblia* available, according to Plato

(*Ap.* 26d), for a drachma in the Athenian marketplace: "Summary pronouncements of the philosopher's doctrine . . . compressed in style and even oracular and . . . published as a guide to the philosopher's system to be used as a supplement to oral teaching." Both points—the summary character of the texts and the contrast between them and their oral counterparts—are crucial to the view of early *technē* taken here. Contrast A. Gercke, "Die alte Τέχνη Ῥητορική und ihre Gegner," *Hermes* 33 (1897): 348–59, who argues, correctly it seems to me, for the absence of precept from the early rhetorical manuals, but believes that the texts they contained were actual performance texts, to be memorized and repeated word for word.

13. Conceivably Aristotle is here using *technē* to refer to what was "technically rigorous" (*entechnon:* cf. *Rhet.* 1.1 1354a13 and 1355a4) in Corax's book. But this would be a very unusual meaning for the term and is fairly well excluded if the similar remark at *Rhet.* 2.23 140015–16 (to be discussed later in this chapter) is taken as a reference to the "earlier" *technē* of Theodorus rather than to *technē* "before" Theodorus. An "earlier *technē*" could hardly be anything but an actual book or chapter in a book.

14. Democritus (B 278) and Herodotus (8.83.2) use the word *katastasis* in conjunction with and, presumably, contrast with *physis* (human physical nature) to designate regular or long-standing aspects of the human condition, both times in a context where conscious planning and decision are about to intervene—just as they would in a case at law—to modify those existing states of affairs. The same meaning and context reappear in the Protagorean title (80 A 8b) "The State of Affairs (*katastasis*) in the Beginning"—if, as is usually assumed, the *katastasis* is the one described in Plato's Protagoras myth. The word comes eventually to be a virtual synonym for that one among the canonical parts of an oration which supplies necessary information about the *katastasis* of a case—rhetorical *narratio* (see D. A. Russell, *Greek Declamation* [Cambridge, 1983], 88, n. 6). The (also Ionic) meaning that Russell cites from the Hippocratean *Epidemics* ("the general climatic conditions which are the background to a particular outbreak of illness"), is quite close, however, to the one suggested.

15. The model character of the passage does not preclude, of course, the possibility of its containing a serious effort to deal with the general problem involved. For an analysis of Thrasymachus's views on civil strife, see E. A. Havelock, *The Liberal Temper in Greek Politics* (New Haven, Conn., 1957), 230–39.

16. For the nature of the procedures illustrated by Evenus of Paros, see B. Gentili, *Poetry and Its Public in Ancient Greece* (Eng. tr., Baltimore, 1988), 110.

17. Further subdivision under the rubrics of "proper," "compound," "cognate" (*adelpha*), and "epithets" is possible; but the attribution of these terms to Licymnius rests on the late testimony of Hermias's commentary to *Phaedrus* 267c (p. 239.12 = B XVI 2).

18. Sharp separation of narrative from proof makes its first appearance in the dicanic speeches of Isocrates (17.2–4; 18.11–12; 19.16; 21.3–4); the distinct, effective peroration in Demosthenes. Th. Miller, though he searches for traces of the Theodectean tetrad in all the Euripidean speeches he classifies as dicanic, finds narratives less than half as frequent as proems (*Euripides rhetoricus* [Göttingen, 1887]). A similar search in Aristophanes leads C. T. Murphy to observe: "It must be admitted that occasionally only the beginning of a speech shows any flavor of rhetoric," "a full narrative diegesis seldom occurs," and "*epilogos* is less regular in its appearance" ("Aristophanes and the Art of Rhetoric," *Harv. Stud. Class. Phil.* 49 [1938]: 81, 82, and 83).

19. Ignorance of the method is, of course, explicitly attested to by Aristotle if one translates, as many scholars do, "the whole of *technē* before Theodorus" rather than "the whole of the earlier *technē* of Theodorus." Either interpretation is preferable to supposing that Thrasymachus, Theodorus's immediate predecessor in most lists of earlier *technē*, introduced a division into speech components that was ignored by Theodorus in his earlier writings, to be resuscitated (with a vengeance) in his later ones. This reconstruction is certainly possible, but there is nothing in the testimony about Thrasymachus to make us prefer it to the simpler, more economical one first suggested.

20. The attainment of these qualities was doubtless one of the things promised by the authors of the typical *technē*—hence the possibility that the Anonymus echoes their language in his introduction, even though one of the purposes of his discussion is to show that memorizing the contents of a *technē* is not in itself sufficient to allow the student to achieve his goal. Character formation, according to him, begins early in life and the reputation for honesty thus accumulated over many years is of more consequence.

21. The parallels between the passages discussed in this and the following paragraph were first pointed out in F. Heinimann, "Eine vorplatonische Theorie der τέχνη," *MusHelv* 18 (1961): 105–30.

22. Cf. P. Shorey, "Φύσις, Μελέτη, Ἐπιστήμη," *TAPA* 40 (1909): 185–94 (= *Selected Papers* [New York, 1980], 1:2–11).

23. For an attempt—unconvincing, in my view—to attribute its incorporation into the rhetorical *technē* to Theodectes, see H. Blum, *Die antike Mnemotechnik* (Hildesheim, 1969), 80–104.

24. The earliest attested use of the word *topos* with a specifically rhetorical or philosophical meaning (Isoc. *Helen* 3–4) is in reference to the paradoxes of Gorgias and the Eleatics.

25. Aristotle, for example, is anything but clear when he says that a *topos* is "that into the category of which a number of *enthymemes* fall" (*Rhet.* 2.26 1403a18–19). And yet, "so knapp diese Bemerkung ist, ist sie merkwürdigerweise doch die einzige authentische Aüsserung des Aristoteles über das Wesen des *topos*" (F. Solmsen, *Die Entwicklung des aristotelischen Logik und Rhetorik* [Berlin, 1929], 164).

26. For *epideixis* as oral presentation of what has been prepared beforehand, either through writing or careful rehearsal, see also Isoc. 5.17, 26, and 93; and Arist., *Rhet.* 3.12 1414a17 (the epideictic style as a written style). It is presumably just such an *epideixis* that Phaedrus is planning when he is forced to "exhibit" (*deiknuein* [228d6–e2]) to Socrates the actual physical document rather than the version of it he has been memorizing and practicing.

Chapter 6 The Range and Limits of Technē

1. See, for an earlier critique of this view, S. Wilcox, "The Scope of Early Rhetorical Instruction," *Harv. Stud. Class. Phil.* 53 (1942): 122–55.

2. For this interpretation of the terms *brachylogia* and *makrologia* see G. B. Kerferd, *The Sophistic Movement* (Cambridge, 1981), 32–33.

3. Compare Plato, *Phaedr.* 271c1–2, on "the contemporary writers of *logōn technai*" that Phaedrus has heard of, with Isocrates, *Against the Sophists* 19–20, on "writers of an earlier generation responsible for the so-called *technai*" that promised mastery of dicanic *logoi*.

4. The encomium of Heracles is, of course, the piece preserved in Xenophon's *Memorablia* (see chapter 5). On the probable contents of the praise of agriculture, see A. Henrichs, "The Sophists and Hellenistic Religion," *Harv. Stud. Class. Phil.* 86 (1984): 140–45.

5. Cf. R. Kassel, "Untersuchungen zur griechischen und römischen Konsolationsliteratur," *Zetemata* 18 (1958): 9–10. Antiphon's text probably began, in typical *technē* fashion, with an *epangelma;* cf. A6: "Antiphon . . . advertised (*epēngeile*) 'pain-relieving lectures' (*nēpentheis akroaseis*), maintaining that no-one could name a grief so great that they would not put it out of his mind." It may have been as much for display as for demonstration—if the richness of detail and stylistic polish shown in B49 were sustained throughout. But this does not exclude, any more than it does in Gorgias's *Helen,* an ultimately practical purpose.

6. Cf. Plato's reference (*Phaedr.* 261bc) to the *technai* composed by "Nes-

tor" (Gorgias) and "Odysseus" (Thrasymachus) during their sojourn at Troy.

7. On the dialect and probable date of the *Twofold Arguments*, see T. M. Robinson, *Contrasting Arguments, an Edition of the* Dissoi Logoi (New York, 1979).

8. "A second-level sophistic *epideixis* . . . an artificial defence of Athenian policy against a perhaps slightly less artificial attack." G. Forrest, "An Athenian Generation Gap," *YClS* 24 (1975): 45.

9. A. W. Gomme, "The Old Oligarch," *Harv. Stud. Class. Phil.* Suppl. 1 (1940): 211.

10. Glen Bowersock, "The Pseudo-Xenophontic *Constitution of the Athenians*," *Harv. Stud. Class. Phil.* 71 (1966): 33–38.

11. R. Sealey, "The Origin of Demokratia," *California Studies in Classical Antiquity* 6 (1973): 260–62.

12. E. Schwartz, *Das Geschichtswerk des Thukydides*, 2d ed. (Bonn, 1929), 102.

13. The elaborate and detailed series of contrasts between the two passages is noted and analyzed by Günther Wille, "Zu Stil und Methode des Thukydides," in *Synusia, Festgabe für Wolfgang Schadewaldt* (Pfullingen, 1965), 57–77 = Hans Herter, ed., *Thukydides, Wege der Forschung* xcviii (Darmstadt, 1968), 700–716.

14. See, for example, Wilamowitz, *Aristoteles und Athen* (Berlin, 1893), 1, 171–85.

15. The unlikelihood of this view was demonstrated, on the basis of detailed comparison with datable passages in Euripides and Sophocles, by J. H. Finley, Jr., "Euripides and Thucydides" *Harv. Stud. Class. Phil.* 49 (1938): 7–49, and "The Origins of Thucydides' Style," *Harv. Stud. Class. Phil.* 50 (1939): 67–89 (= *Three Essays on Thucydides* [Cambridge, Mass., 1967], 1–117).

16. For this view of the speeches as "instruments of conveying the tendencies of society and human nature on which alone foresight is based," and so the "main means of presenting the compelling forces in the history of the time," see J. H. Finley, *Thucydides* (Cambridge, Mass., 1942), 96–100.

17. For such indications in the speeches of Alcibiades and Nicias in Book 6, see Daniel Tompkins, "Stylistic Characterization in Thucydides: Nicias and Alcibiades," *YClS* 22 (1972): 181–214.

18. See H.-P. Stahl in P. A. Stadter, ed., *The Speeches of Thucydides* (Chapel Hill, N.C., 1973), 60–76.

19. See, for example, Hunter Rawlings, *The Structure of Thucydides' History* (Princeton, N.J., 1981).

20. The result is—not surprisingly—a passage "unique in character and style" (D. Kagan, *The Archidamian War* [Ithaca, N.Y., 1974], 241).

Chapter 7 Rhetoric and Prose

1. G. Ryle, *Plato's Progress* (Cambridge, 1961), 203. Ryle's further suggestion (pp. 18 and 203) that portions of these reading texts were actual records of real debates and intended for performance as well as reading—dramatized "case books of recent moots" whose purpose was "to help students remember and digest the argument sequences that finally crystallized out of those moots"—is possible, but much less certain. The Platonic passages which sound like "dramatized Hansards" for an audience are far less numerous than those which sound like fiction for readers.

2. Nearly a fourth of the speeches in the Lysianic corpus fall into this category.

3. In Isaeus 5. See Franz Lämmli, *Das attische Prozessverfahren in seiner Wirkung auf die Gerichtsrede* (Paderborn, 1938), 119, n. 2.

4. Alcidamas is usually dated earlier, to the 390s (see, for example, G. Avezzù, *Alcidamante, Orazioni e frammenti* [Rome, 1981], 71), on the basis of parallels with Isocratean works (*Helen, Contra Soph., Paneg.*) composed between 400 and 380. But the parallels are so general that direct, immediate influence of one author on the other need not be involved. The parallels with Plato's *Phaedrus* are, by contrast, much closer, and would suggest a date in the 360s (cf. below, n. 12).

5. See the passages assembled and discussed by K. Barwick, "Das Problem der isokrateischen Techne," *Philologus* 107 (1963): 42–60.

6. Theopompus is the most conspicuous example: more "prosecutor" than "recorder" of events, according to Lucian (*Quomodo historia scribenda sit,* 59). Cf. the generally concurring assessment of W. R. Connor, *Theopompus and Fifth-Century Athens* (Washington, D.C., 1958), 121–24.

7. See the discussion in B. Gentili and G. Cerri, *Storia e biografia nel pensiero antico* (Bari, 1983), 12–17.

8. On written discourse as artifact, see the discussion in E. A. Havelock, *The Greek Concept of Justice* (Cambridge, Mass., 1978), 221 ff.

9. Antisthenes had recourse to the same analogy in introducing his notion (see chapter 4) of Odysseus as a master of the various ways (*tropoi*) of conveying the same thought (*noēma*). He compares the *tropoi* of a given *logos* to modulations of the voice in speaking or singing.

10. R. Barthes, *Le plaisir du texte* (Paris, 1973), 22–23.

11. Two central Isocratean tenets—the necessity of fitting style to subject matter and part to whole—may in fact have arisen through an effort to find some written counterpart to the performer's ability to vary his presentation according to the *kairos* of a given occasion. See M. Vallozza, "Καιρός nella teoria retorica di Alcidamante e di Isocrate,

ovvero nell' oratoria orale e scritta," *Quaderni Urbinati* 50 (1985): 119 ff.

12. The *Busiris* is generally dated to near the beginning of the writer's career (c. 390 B.C.; cf. R. C. Jebb, *The Greek Orators from Antiphon to Isaeus* (Cambridge, 1886), 2:94–95). The *Helen* is so similar that one would expect it to have been written around the same time, though it is, presumably, later than the death of Gorgias (c. 380 B.C.). The late dating of the *Phaedrus* (some time in the 360s rather than the 390s) is now generally accepted (see, for example, the commentaries of Hackforth and DeVries).

13. See R. L. Howland, "The Attack on Isocrates in the *Phaedrus*," *Classical Quarterly* 31 (1937): 153.

14. For a similar concern with the propriety of one's evaluations in the *Busiris*, see 40 (one should not be allowed to speak ill of the gods), 44 (Busiris's crimes must not be excused simply because others are guilty of the same thing or worse), 47 (praise of men for evil deeds is best if it fails to convince the audience).

15. For example, concern for "truth" versus concern for pleasure and display at 12.271, the accuracy (*akribeia*) required for private themes versus the epideictic manner needed for larger ones at 4.11, style and sound versus truth at 5.4, the fanciful versus the useful at 2.48.

16. The *Rhetorica ad Alexandrum*, although dating from the 330s and indebted to what seem to be Platonic or Aristotelian sources at many points, is more "primitive" than the *Phaedrus* in this respect: all of its numerous and extensive illustrative examples are, so far as one can tell, the work of the author himself.

17. Collected in V. Rose, *Aristotelis fragmenta*, 2d ed. (Leipzig, 1886), 114–18.

18. Cf., for example, the comment in Kennedy (56): "Socrates has begun with the contents of the proemium and passed through the traditional parts of a judicial speech, the narration, the subdivisions of the proof and the epilogue."

19. An epitome of the *technē* of Theodectes appears in the list of Aristotelian titles preserved by Diogenes Laertius (5.25), and some assume that this is identical with the work in question. See, for example, F. Solmsen, "Drei Rekonstruktionen zur antiken Rhetorik und Poetik," *Hermes* 67 (1932): 146–51 (= *Kleine Schriften* 2.140–47), followed by P. Moraux, *Les Listes anciennes des ouvrages d'Aristote* (Louvain, 1951), 98–101. Aristotle himself, however, speaks of *ta Theodekteia*, a form of reference normally reserved in Aristotelian treatises for the philosopher's own works (see E. M. Cope, *An Introduction to Aristotle's Rhetoric* [London, 1867], 22). Nor is it even certain that an epitome of Theodectes written by Aristotle existed at all. See note 20, below, and,

for a survey of the relevant scholarship, H. A. Chroust, "Aristotle's Earliest Course of Lectures on Rhetoric," *Aristotle* (London, 1973), 2:109–13.

20. So V. Rose (*Aristoteles Pseudepigraphus* [Leipzig, 1863], 135), who paraphrases τέχνης ῥητορικῆς Θεοδεκτικὴ συναγωγή. His interpretation is also supported by the fact that a compendium is normally a "bringing together" of the substance of an entire discipline or of several individual works, not an epitome of a single one. Either interpretation is grammatically possible, depending on whether the possessive *Theodektou* in the phrase τέχνης τῆς Θεοδέκτου συναγωγῆς is taken as dependent on *technēs* or *synagōgē*. Other manuscripts and other versions of the list have *synagōgē* in the nominative or accusative, which would require the first interpretation. But an original genitive could easily have been altered by a copyist who assumed, quite reasonably, that anything included in a catalogue of Aristotle's works was more likely to be by Aristotle than by Theodectes.

21. The polymath is often assumed to be Heraclides Ponticus, but with no very good reason: see H. B. Gottschalk, *Heraclides of Pontus* (Oxford, 1980), 159–60.

22. "So kann mit μόνος kaum etwas anderes angedeutet werden als dass Theodektes selbst nicht τὴν τέχνην ἀνηῦρε." Karl Barwick, "Die Gliederung des rhetorischen τέχνη und die horazische Epistula ad Pisones," *Hermes* (1922): 24.

23. διηγήσομαι ὑμῖν ὡς ἂν δύνωμαι διὰ βραχυτάτων (Isoc. 21.2; cf. 19.4 and Lysias 12.3 and 24.4). It is hard to see any other reason for requiring all narrative to have brevity as one of its qualities. Cf. the critique in Aristotle (*Rhet.* 3.16 1416b29–17a2).

24. Cf. Lysias 13.2 (δεῖ δ' ὑμᾶς ἐξ ἀρχῆς τῶν πραγμάτων ἁπάντων ἀκοῦσαι); 1.5; 7.3; 12.3; 32.3; Isoc. 18.4 (βούλομαι δ' ἐξ αρχῆς διηγήσασθαι τὰ πράγματα); 17.3. Though not ascribed specifically to Theodectes, the rule is criticized by Aristotle (*Rhet.* 3.16 1416b16–23) in much the same way as the Theodectean call for brevity. For clarity as a virtue of narrative (fr. 126), cf. Isoc. 17.2 (ἡγοῦμαι πᾶσι φανερὸν ποιῆσαι) and Lysias 13.4 (ὅθεν οὖν ἡμεῖς τε ῥᾶστα διδάξομεν καὶ ὑμεῖς μαθήσεσθε, ἐντεῦθεν ἄρξομαι ὑμῖν διηγεῖσθαι).

25. For later examples of both types, see Barwick, "Die Gliederung," 11–14.

26. Cf. Aristotle's recipe (see chapter 1) for composing a tragedy (*Poet.* 17 1455a34–55b12). Similar procedures are attributed to Menander (Plut., *De glor. Athen.* 4.347e–f: blocking out of the whole action of a play beforehand, followed a day or two before the premiere by words and verses) and to Virgil (*Vita Donati* 22: composition of the *Aeneid* bit by bit, in no fixed order, but on the basis of a prose summary, divided into books, that was written out beforehand).

Chapter 8 Rhetoric and Philosophy

1. See, for the *Republic,* the analysis in E. A. Havelock, *A Preface to Plato* (Oxford, 1963), 36 ff.
2. See H. Cherniss, "The Philosophical Economy of the Theory of Ideas," *American Journal of Philology* 57 (1936): 445–46 (= *Selected Papers* [Leiden, 1971], 121–22).
3. Encomium and hymn are the two genres referred to in Plato, *Rep.* 10.607a, where all types of narrative or dramatic representation are rejected as conducive to a failure to distinguish reality from imitation. The other formulation comes from *Rep.* 3.396c–e, where the emphasis is more moral than intellectual: the deterioration of character that comes from portraying, or observing others portray, weak and evil men.
4. The particular version of past events presented in the *Menexenus* may well be, as has often been assumed, a parody of the patriotic distortions that were a part of festival rhetoric at Athens. But the conclusion the reader should draw from this need be no more than that fifth-century Athenian history, however distorted, is ill suited to inspire feelings of patriotism, not that public reporting of it should be more accurate. Plato's own excursions into the history of his city at an earlier period (*Timaeus* 24d–25d, *Critias* 108e) are far more fanciful than anything attributed to Aspasia in the *Menexenus.*
5. See L. Taràn, "The Creation Myth in Plato's *Timaeus,*" in J. P. Anton and G. L. Kustas, eds., *Studies in Ancient Philosophy* (Albany, N.Y., 1972), 388–90.
6. The vital role played by metaphor in early Greek scientific speculation has been stressed by G. E. R. Lloyd, *The Revolutions of Wisdom: Studies in the Claims and Practice of Ancient Greek Science* (Berkeley, 1987), 203–14.
7. Nonlovers, unfaithful wives, and cannibalistic kings are the objects of the encomiums in, respectively, Lysias's speech in the *Phaedrus,* Gorgias's *Helen,* and the work of Polycrates discussed in the *Busiris.* Salt (cf., also, Plato, *Symp.* 177b) and mud are mentioned as encomium topics in Isoc. *Helen* 12.
8. Isoc. 12.2, 13.6, 15.183, *Ep.* 6.8 (*topoi*); 10.15, 11.33 (figures of speech); 15.46 (literary genres). For the Democritean usage, see B167 and A 135.
9. All could be called *logoi* in Greek, for which the best single translation in such contexts is perhaps that implied by the title of F. Solmsen's study, *Intellectual Experiments of the Greek Enlightenment* (Princeton, N.J., 1975).

10. This is, for example, the view of Gorgias taken by T. G. Rosenmeyer, "Gorgias, Aeschylus and Apate," *American Journal of Philology* 76 (1955): 231–32.

11. See, for the view of Protagoras presented here, my discussion in "The Relativism of Protagoras," *YClS* 22 (1971): 33–35. Most scholars interpret the better *logos* rather differently—as the more useful one or the one more in accord with "normal" human attitudes; but if their views are correct, Protagoras would have been even less inclined to countenance the unrestrained use of persuasive techniques that is usually attributed to the Sophists.

12. This is the thesis, for example, of J. de Romilly, *Magic and Rhetoric in Ancient Greece* (Cambridge, 1975), 3–22, developed from the earlier studies of Rosenmeyer, "Gorgias" and C. P. Segal, "Gorgias and the Psychology of the Logos," *Harv. Stud. Class. Phil.* 66 (1962): 99–155.

13. This is true, if, as is usually assumed, Gorgias is thinking of written compositions to be read or recited from memory before a jury. It is conceivable, however, that he has epideictic eloquence in mind—as the reference to writing (see chapter 5) and to delighting as well as persuading an audience might suggest. In that case the passage is even less indicative of the sort of role Gorgias assigned to *technē* in the general process of audience persuasion.

14. Cf. B 3 *bis.* 21–25 U. There, having granted for the sake of argument that it is possible for the perception on which a verbal message is based to be both accurate and identical in the mind of message-sender and message-recipient, Gorgias goes on to argue that there is nevertheless nothing to prevent (*ouden kōluei*) the thing's *appearing* dissimilar to the two persons—just as even the same person's impressions of the same thing are not always consistent from one moment to the next. This formulation seems, at any rate, to allow for the alternative possibility as well: that there is "nothing to prevent" the content of a message "appearing" similar to both sender and recipient and so similar to the "being" on whose perception it was originally based.

15. Another witness to the process of transition is, presumably, the *Rhetorica ad Alexandrum,* which contains a certain amount of unquestionably Aristotelian material that may be roughly contemporary with the earliest portions of the *Rhetoric*. But the *Entstehungsgeschichte* of this rhetorical treatise is even harder to unravel than that of Aristotle's own.

16. The view of the relationship between *topos* and *protasis* taken in the text follows, in general, Friedrich Solmsen, *Die Entwicklung der aristotelischen Logik und Rhetorik, Neue Philologische Untersuchungen* 4 (1929), 209–29.

17. As Theophrastus in fact sought to do for the *a fortiori topos* (reported in Alexander Aphr. *ad* Arist., *An. Pr.* 1, p. 265 Wallies).

18. Cf., especially, Arist., *An. Pr.* 2.23–24 and 27, with *Rhet.* 1.2 1356b5– 10 and 1357a22–58a2.

19. See, for a brief summary of the evidence, J. L. Stocks, "The Composition of Aristotle's Logical Works," *Classical Quarterly* 27 (1933); 115– 24.

20. The view goes back to Adolf Kantelhardt, *De Aristotelis rhetoricis*, Diss. Göttingen, 1911 (reprinted in Rudolf Stark, ed., *Rhetorica* [Hildesheim, 1968], 124–83).

21. See, for example, F. Solmsen, "The Discovery of the Syllogism," *Philosophical Review* 50 (1941): 410.

22. Compare, in poetics, Aristotle's redefinition of *mimesis* to include narrative as well as dramatic discourse (see chapter 1). The determining consideration in Plato is the imitative character of the poetic medium or signifier (dramatic speech and action representing real speech and action); for Aristotle it is the character of the poetic content or signified—the degree to which the events acted out or narrated are similiar to those that occur in real life.

General Index

ad hominem argumentation: in
rhetoric, 7–9, 49, 133, 159n.5; in
Socratic dialogues, 125
advertising, 22
Aeschylus: and Euripides in the *Frogs*,
62–63, 68; *Seven against Thebes* as
characterized by Gorgias and
Aristophanes, 65–66
Aesop, 49, 60
agōn, as speech part, 82–83
ainos, 49, 60
Ajax, as speaker, 43
akribeia, 74, 126
Alcidamas, date of, 171n.4
Alexander Numeniu, 14
allegory: in Alcaeus and Archilochus,
164n.10; in fifth-century prose,
58–62; in interpretation of the
poets, 56, 67; and rhetoric, 56–57,
67
amplification, 59; as *topos* and subject
for *protaseis* in the *Rhetoric*, 155
analogical reasoning, as *topos* in the
Rhetoric, 156–57
Anaxagoras, *biblia* of, 168–69n.12
Anaximenes of Lampsacus(?), relation
of, to Plato and Aristotle, 177n.15
Andocides, *On the Mysteries*, 117

anger, arousing and assuaging of, 84,
145
Anonymus Iamblichi, 86
Antiphon the "orator": style of, 73;
Tetralogies of, 75, 77–78, 97–98
Antiphon the "Sophist," 100
Antisthenes: on Homer as allegorist,
58; on Odyssean tropes, 58, 173n.9
apoplanēseis, 84
architecture, poetry compared to, 36
Areopagus, 101
aretai of speech and speech parts,
136
Aristophanes, criticism of poetry in,
62, 65–66
Aristotle: as compiler and epitomizer,
129–36; contents of *Rhetoric* of,
10–12; history of composition of
Rhetoric of, 57–57; on the nature of
protorhetoric, 23–27; and Plato's
Phaedrus, 10–12, 153; rhetorical
character of his view of poetry,
15–18, 65, 141; and Thucydides,
109–10. *See also* Plato and Aristotle
arrangement (*dispositio, diathesis,
taxis*): attention to, in early *technē*,
23, 24–25, 82–85; conception of,
in ancient theory, 12, 13, 18–19; in

muse(s), and memory, 34
myth: allegorization of, 56–62;
cosmological and eschatological in
Plato, 140–41; as form of rhetoric,
161n.25; of *Phaedrus*, 8–9

narrative (*narratio*): dramatic plot as
form of, 17; in early oratory, 73,
116–17; in speeches of Odysseus,
39. *See also* arrangement
neorhetoric, 19–22, 163n.2
Nestor, as speaker, 36, 43
newness, as virtue of poetry, 33–36
nomos. *See* contract
"non-rhetorical" discourse, 12, 15, 29,
52, 65–66, 68
non-Western societies, rhetoric in, 48

Odysseus: as master of tropes, 58; as
narrator, 38–39; as speaker, 39–40,
43, 49
oratory: character of, in late fifth
century, 71–73; evolution of, in
early fourth century, 116–18
orthoepeia, 65–66
overcoding, 57
ozoi, 85

paignion, 78
painting, and poetry, 35–36
palillogia, 96
Pamphilus, 83, 97
paradoxes, rhetorical and
philosophical, 143
paraphrase, 21, 42, 165n.8. *See also*
variation
Parmenides, proem of, as rhetoric, 59
parts (*merē*) of speech and discourse,
131. *See also* arrangement
pathos, 4, 10–11, 12, 18, 144–45, 147
Perelmann, Chaim, 20
performance, 37, 41. *See also* texts
Pericles, 77–78, 118
personification, 58–59, 163n.4
persuasion: in Gorgias, 146–53; in
Homer, 39–40; in Pindar, 53; in
Platonic and Aristotelian definitions
of rhetoric, 3
Pherecydes of Athens, 102
Phrynichos, *Sack of Miletus,* 166n.15

Pindar, rhetoric in, 49–53
pity: evocation of, in *Eleoi* of
Thrasymachus, 8, 144–45; and fear,
16
plain style, 65–66
Plato: as creator of rhetorical analysis,
91–93, 129–32; on Gorgianic
rhetoric, 148, 150–52; illustrations
and discussions of rhetoric in, 2–10;
Isocratean influence on, 127–28; on
poetry, 34–35; on writing and
written texts, 121–32, 139
Plato and Aristotle: on early writers of
technē, 23–27, 95; as inventors of
rhetoric, 27–29, 139–41, 157–58;
on the Sophists, 25–26
plausibility, in poetry, 39
plot in drama, 15–16. *See also* content
poetry: as creation and mimesis, 38;
and history according to Aristotle,
17–18; as rhetoric, 27–28, 140;
as source of information, 34–35,
65
poiētēs, 38, 41
Polus, 22, 85
Polycrates, 140
practice (*meletē, epimeleia*): as
prerequisite for success, 88; texts
composed for, 75–83
praise: of Athens, 168n.8; character of,
in Pindaric epinician, 51–53; of salt
and mud, 176n.7
praise and blame: in epic and gnomic
poetry, 85; "indirect," 164n.9
praise and blame, models of, 75, 119;
in Plato and Isocrates, 140; in
Prodicus, 100; before
unsympathetic audiences, 103–4
prefaces to *technē*, probable contents
of, 85–88
prepon. *See* decorum
Prodicus: allegory in, 59; on divine
personifications, 58–59; on
synonyms, 100; three- and forty-
drachma lectures of, 76–77
proem, models for reflected in Attic
oratory, 84–85. *See also*
arrangement
proof (*pistis*), 85. *See also* arrangement
propaganda, 22

Index of Passages Cited

ANCIENT SOCIETY AND HISTORY

The series Ancient Society and History offers books, relatively brief in compass, on selected topics in the history of ancient Greece and Rome, broadly conceived, with a special emphasis on comparative and other nontraditional approaches and methods. The series, which includes both works of synthesis and works of original scholarship, is aimed at the widest possible range of specialist and nonspecialist readers.